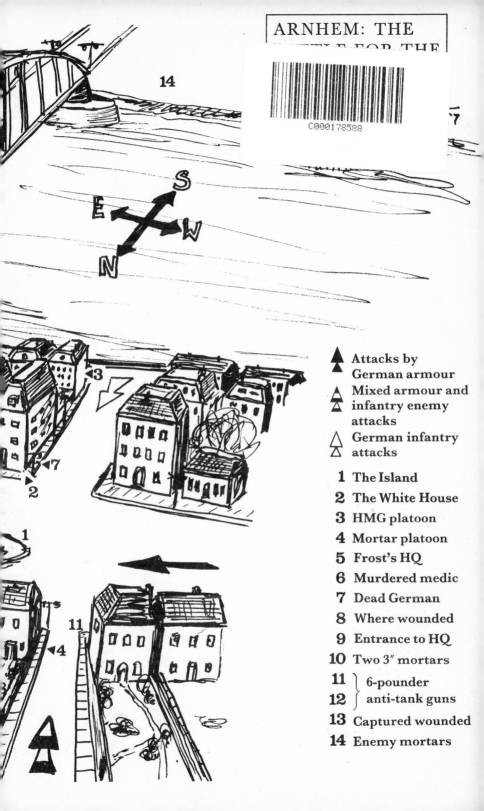

ARNHEM: THE
~~TTLE FOR THE~~

C000178588

14

7

2

Attacks by
German armour

Mixed armour and
infantry enemy
attacks

German infantry
attacks

1 The Island
2 The White House
3 HMG platoon
4 Mortar platoon
5 Frost's HQ
6 Murdered medic
7 Dead German
8 Where wounded
9 Entrance to HQ
10 Two 3″ mortars
11 } 6-pounder
12 } anti-tank guns
13 Captured wounded
14 Enemy mortars

Arnhem Spearhead

Arnhem Spearhead

JAMES SIMS

A private soldier's story

Imperial War Museum

Published by the Imperial War Museum
Lambeth Road, London, SE1 6HZ

© James Sims 1978
Foreword © Major-General J. D. Frost 1978
Introduction © Trustees of the Imperial War Museum 1978

First impression March 1978
Second impression August 1978

ISBN 0 901627 10 0

Printed in Great Britain
by W & J Mackay Limited, Chatham

CONTENTS

ILLUSTRATIONS

Author's Note

I wish to acknowledge the help I have received from the Director of the Imperial War Museum, Dr Noble Frankland, and Dr Christopher Dowling and his staff in the preparation and publication of this book.

James Sims
Brighton
13 September 1977

FOREWORD

by Major-General J D Frost CB DSO MC

THIS IS the first book that I have read which was written by one of the soldiers who trained for and fought at the Battle of Arnhem Bridge in September 1944. It is a most vivid moving personal account which should be of great interest to all kinds of people, for there are few such written by young soldiers either about the last war or any other war for that matter.

It brings back many memories for me, some of which I would rather forego. Yet I feel very grateful to James Sims for reminding us of the fortitude, faith, gallantry and guts displayed by literally all those who were there. He describes so well the atmosphere in the cellars where the wounded lay and tells us of the devotion of the 'medics', both in bringing the wounded in and mitigating their sufferings thereafter. The later chapters about life in captivity are I think unique. Much of the discomfort we all suffered was due to the unexpected influx of so many wounded prisoners at a time when the Germans were nearing the end of their tether. The attitude and bearing of the captured and wounded were outstanding throughout and this helped us mutually to overcome the disappointment, frustration and humiliation which were our lot.

I hope that members of the Royal Regiment of Artillery will not take amiss some of the remarks at the beginning of the book for all of us will be eternally grateful for their support in the battle. The professional skill of the forward elements who were with us could be matched only by the resolution of the Sappers who came, together with headquarters of the 1st Parachute Brigade, Freddie Gough and part of his Reconnaissance Squadron, Peter Lewis and C Company of the 3rd Battalion, and a platoon of the RASC.

There are some errors of description and fact, for the individual soldier's viewpoint is inevitably restricted. However, I am sure it would be a mistake to niggle over these for to do so might spoil the flow of the narrative. The reader will want to feel that the descriptions are exactly as the soldier saw them at the time and as he remembers them now.

Nevertheless I feel I must say that I am sure the author is wrong in asserting that the soldiers who brought the wounded out of the burning building (page 85) were other than troops of the 9th SS Panzer Division. Although at times these men were a bit 'quick on the draw', during our battle they were a chivalrous foe. Their sympathy and kindness for us wounded I, for one, will not forget.

As you progress with James Sims through the chapters of his book, you should be able to say, at the end, 'I begin to see what makes the British soldier tick.'

INTRODUCTION

MANY BOOKS have been written about the battle of Arnhem by
the senior commanders and more junior officers involved in
that disastrous but heroic engagement. Here for the first time is
the story of the battle, or rather of its vortex – the struggle for
the bridge – as seen through the eyes of a private soldier. After
volunteering for the Parachute Regiment and successfully com-
pleting the rigorous training necessary to qualify for admission
to this *corps d'élite* James Sims in September 1944, at the age of
nineteen, found himself a participant in the greatest airborne
assault in the history of warfare – Operation Market Garden – a
daring airborne and ground offensive designed to blast a 'back-
door' route through Holland into the industrial heart of Germany. His unit, the 2nd Battalion The Parachute Regiment,
formed part of the vanguard of the formidable 1st British Airborne Division. Its able and experienced commander, Lieutenant-
Colonel John Frost, was given the crucial task of seizing the
massive high-arched bridge which spanned the Lower Rhine at
Arnhem.

Frost's battalion reached its objective as dusk was falling on
Sunday 17 September only to discover that the southern end of
the bridge was strongly held by the enemy. The Germans reacted to the British landings with characteristic speed and
determination. Allied intelligence reports indicating the presence
of two German armoured divisions in the Arnhem area had
been brushed aside by over-confident British commanders. As
the author relates, he and his companions had expected to
encounter only a handful of dispirited 'ear and stomach' battalions. Instead, the lightly armed and equipped paratroopers
met fierce resistance from some of the toughest troops in the
German Army – the seasoned veterans of the 9th and 10th SS
Panzer Divisions – supported by tanks, self-propelled guns and

artillery. Cut off from the rest of the 1st Airborne Division and
from the tanks of the British Second Army struggling to break
through to them from the south, the 2nd Battalion and elements
of other units clung to the northern end of the bridge for three
days and four nights against almost ceaseless attacks by German
armour and panzer grenadiers. When they were finally over-
whelmed on the morning of 21 September fewer than 200
haggard, exhausted, yet still-defiant men remained out of the
original force of more than 700; many, including the author
and his CO, were wounded.

James Sims describes what he graphically terms this 'physical
and spiritual auto-da-fe' in simple, terse and vivid prose. He
writes unsentimentally and yet with genuine compassion for
both friend and foe alike. In particular he paints an unforgettable picture of the selfless courage and grim humour of his
comrades as, powerless to defend themselves against the German
armour and with only a few rounds of ammunition left, they
waited for the end in an inferno of fumes and dust and falling
masonry. He concludes his narrative with a remarkable account
of his experiences as a prisoner of war in Germany during the
final chaotic months of the Third Reich. His book, which is in
the tradition of Rifleman Harris and George Coppard, will
surely become a classic of the Second World War.

As General Frost points out, there are some errors of detail.
For example, the pontoon bridge mentioned on pages 42 and 44
was built by the Dutch, not by German Army engineers, and it
was never blown: the Germans rendered it useless by destroying
the centre section. On page 82 there is a reference to a major
(who would have been Freddie Gough) wearing 'the grey beret
and spearhead badge of the Reconnaissance Corps'. All members
of the Reconnaissance Squadron, which was an integral part of
the Parachute Regiment, wore the red beret. The 'SS von
Clausewitz Panzer Division' (page 115) was not an SS formation
but a scratch unit assembled from the staff and students of a
panzer training school near Uelzen. It was destroyed not by the
British but by the tanks and guns of the American Ninth Army.
These and other minor inaccuracies add to rather than detract
from the authenticity of *Arnhem Spearhead*, since they show that

the author has relied on his own impressions and experiences and has not adulterated his account by bringing it into line with other sources.

We should like to record our indebtedness to the distinguished military historian, Professor Michael Howard, our colleague on the Museum's Publication Board, who is also a Trustee of the Museum. In addition our thanks are due to Major-General Frost for contributing the Foreword. It must be unusual – if not unique – for a book written by a private to carry a foreword by a general. A leading Dutch authority on Arnhem, Dr Adrian Groeneweg, kindly read the manuscript and made a number of helpful comments. The preliminary editorial work was undertaken by the late Mr Vernon Rigby, formerly of the Museum's Department of Education and Publications.

Arnhem Spearhead is the fourth title in the Museum's series of personal reminiscences of the two world wars and the first to be published in hardback under the Museum's own imprint. It is also the first Second World War narrative to appear in the series. The three previous volumes, all of which were published in paperback by HMSO, were *Across the Piave*, *To the Ends of the Air* and the highly acclaimed *With a Machine Gun to Cambrai*.

Noble Frankland
Director of the Imperial War Museum

Christopher Dowling
Keeper of the Department of Education and Publications

22 September 1977

Chapter 1

TRAINING FOR THE HIGH JUMP

WHEN THE Second World War started I was still at school in Brighton. In 1941 I joined the Army Cadet Corps and in 1942 the Home Guard. In January 1943 I volunteered for the Army; at that time I was still under eighteen years of age. I completed almost a year at Larkhill on Salisbury Plain with the 4th Field Training Regiment, Royal Artillery, and didn't much care for it.

If you had any spirit at all the RA seemed determined to break it. Their attitude has been summed up as follows:

If it moves – salute it!
If it stands still – blanco it!
If it's too heavy to lift – paint it!

Two Manchester lads and myself decided that we'd had enough and the visit of a Parachute Regiment recruiting team clinched the matter. They talked about our joining their 'band of brothers'. No one ever referred to you as a brother in the RA, which is no doubt a great regiment, but it was not for us. We could see no future in heaving 25-pounder gun-howitzers about. Either you have this love of inanimate objects or you haven't. We didn't mind fighting, but as one of the Manchester lads, Jack Jolliffe, put it, 'If I'm in action I want to be able to look after myself and not be nursemaid to a bloody great gun.'

We filled in the necessary application forms and had to complete a qualifying course, which included firing a rifle from either shoulder and hitting the bull. Try it some time. We passed all the tests, including a stiff physical, but for some reason Len Davis, the other Manchester lad, couldn't come with us and I believe he eventually joined the 6th Airborne Division. The colonel of the 4th Field Regiment interviewed us before we left and seemed stupefied to learn that two of his men wanted a transfer from the RA and to the 'Umbrella Danglers' at that. We endeavoured to convince him that we were not mad and on 9 February 1944 I was issued with joining instructions in respect of 14419841 Gnr Sims, J. and 1151469 Gnr Jolliffe, J., who were to report to the RTO Chesterfield at 1535 hours that day.

We left Larkhill before reveille, shaking hands with the lads of 23 Squad 'B' Battery before doing so. We arrived at Chesterfield station on time. Outside was a ten-ton troop carrier with a ten-ton airborne sergeant to go with it. A motley collection of soldiers had descended from the train. They were all shapes and sizes, from huge guardsmen to bantam-sized riflemen, and included quick-witted signalmen and slow-moving RAOC storemen. The sergeant grinned and shouted, 'Right, lads. On the truck.' We scrambled aboard, our studded boots scrabbling on the steel floor. One foolish man went up to the huge sergeant and tried to say something. The sergeant picked him and his kitbag up and slung him over the tailboard of the truck to land among us. 'I said get on the bloody truck,' he bellowed.

When we were all on, the sergeant climbed up into the front cab and off we went. 'He must be one of the band of brothers they told us about,' I muttered to Jack. Our journey was a short one and we soon arrived at the Airborne Forces Depot at Hardwick Hall Camp. It was a fair-sized place, flanked by cliffs on one side and a small lake on the other. We were allocated huts and were given a meal; the food was good and you could have as much as you wanted.

As we were all volunteers and dead keen there was a very happy atmosphere and we quickly settled down. We paraded each morning shivering with cold, for all that we were allowed to wear over our vest and pants were denims. We doubled everywhere. Our squad was under a very pugnacious little Army Physical Training Corps sergeant called Bartlett. His nickname was 'Basher'. As he doubled us up hill and down dale he always shouted, 'Bags of steam, boys – give it bags of steam!' He soon had us eating out of his hand because we had already discovered a basic difference between airborne NCOs and those of other regiments and corps. They led by example. If anything tough or rotten had to be done, they did it with you, and usually did it better. Instead of curses you received encouragement.

We were issued with two pamphlets, one of which was a folding card with the maroon and blue Pegasus insignia on it and entitled AIRBORNE FORCES. It began:

> You are now joining Airborne Forces.
> They are something new, different and specialised. They are composed of picked troops. Show by your turn-out, saluting, soldierly bearing and efficiency that you belong to a Corps d'Elite.

The other pamphlet was entitled DISCIPLINE – THE ONLY ROAD TO VICTORY. On page seven, heavily accentuated in black, were the following words:

> The ultimate object of discipline is to ensure that, when things are going badly, casualties have been heavy, leaders have been killed and the troops are 'out on their feet' from strain and exhaustion, then the instinctive reaction in the tired brain and body is: 'Go on – I must keep going' . . . 'Hold on – I must hold on.' That is the final test of whether an army is well-disciplined or not.

Both of these pamplets, issued to each airborne recruit, were written by General Browning, GOC Airborne Forces. These words had a profound effect on me and I never forgot them, especially in training. We used to do a lot of forced marches in battle order and quite a number of men, in particular the heavy smokers, flaked out by the roadside; but no matter how tired I felt I kept on putting one foot in front of the other. 'Go on – I must keep going.' I was six feet tall and weighed eleven stone seven pounds, but I have never had a very robust physique. However, I was determined to succeed. Those who fell out on the march were returned to their units. One thing that did help us during this period was the weather, which was freezing cold, so one was glad to run about and warm up.

One morning as we were leaving the camp an officer stopped us and made us fill our empty ammunition pouches with stones before commencing our one-mile run before breakfast. Another day they took us out to the foot of the cliffs which dominated the camp and which were over one hundred feet in height. We watched without much enthusiasm as six men came down the face of the cliffs on ropes which were secured to large metal stakes on the summit. The method of descent was as follows. After running the rope over your right shoulder and through your legs you leant back on it and placed your feet against the face of the cliff. You then used both hands to pay out the rope while jumping down the cliff face about six feet at a time. It was not difficult but required overwhelming confidence.

One afternoon they took about thirty of us to Hardwick Hall, which was built for Bess of Hardwick, Countess of Shrewsbury, around 1590. It was a most imposing building with a great amount of glass in the front and the old girl's initials, ES, over the gables. In the front porch there was a stone statue of her which I mistook for Queen Elizabeth. They told us we were going to play Paratroop Football, for which the dress was steel helmets, denims, boots and gaiters. There were two goals and no rules and the important thing was to get 'stuck in' to one another. The game lasted for about an hour until there was a cracked collar-bone, a broken arm, no goals on either side because the ball had vanished, but several free fights.

Although it was bitterly cold that February we went out every night and had a damned good time. We usually went to a pub or the pictures and finished up with fish and chips. The fish and chips of Chesterfield are the best I've ever tasted. No one was very late to bed as the training was tough and you had to be fit. If you failed or refused anything you were out.

It was now drawing towards the end of our fortnight at Hardwick. All the physically unfit had been returned to their units. The remainder of us had to go before a psychiatrist or 'trick cyclist' as he was popularly known. Psychiatry was a fairly new thing in the Army at that time and didn't impress us much. One of the questions fired at us was 'Why do you hate your mother?' If you sat there calmly and replied, 'Good heavens, what on earth gave you that idea?' you were out – for lack of aggression. Those who had already been in tipped us off about what to do. You had to put on a show of fury. You had to jump up, knocking the chair over backwards and shout, 'What the hell are you on about?' Better still, you should reach across and make a grab at the psychiatrist. Then you were sure of a rifle company.

The course ended with a series of tests and battle inoculation. We had to wade across rivers, climb walls, crawl through pipes and under barbed wire, walk planks, and cross ravines on ropes whilst thunder-flashes went off all around and machine-gun fire whipped overhead. We finished up attacking imitation German positions on top of the cliff and descending the face of it. All this was carried out in freezing weather. The following day we had to do a ten-mile run in full battle order, but a blizzard started and the conditions were so bad that several men passed out and had to be collected by the medical truck following behind. The blizzard got so bad that the run was called off, but as we had completed seven miles in an hour under adverse conditions it was considered a pass.

On the last Saturday at Hardwick we had a glorious booze-up to celebrate our success so far and began to wonder what Ringway would be like. Ringway Airport, Manchester, was where we had to go to do eight jumps to qualify for the coveted red beret and parachute wings.

We arrived at Ringway on 23 February 1944 and immediately came under RAF discipline, which, after the Army, seemed non-existent. Perhaps it was because the RAF were all specialists of one sort or another, too occupied with their work to bother about foot drill or bull. We were allocated huts and allowed to make our own way to a new mess hall. This was light, noisy and friendly. The food, which was excellent, was served by WAAF girls, who were cheerful and charming. They were always asking us, 'Do you want some more, love?'

The huts were large and comfortable and had built-in loudspeaker systems which broadcast music and news. The RAF also used this system to sound reveille and to alert us for lectures and parades. The first morning we were marched round to the front of some huge hangars where a sort of parade took place. I say 'sort of' because the general standard of drill and marching was appalling. Here we were introduced to the RAF

Sergeant Parachute Instructors who would train us for the next two weeks until we had completed our parachute course. Our instructor was Ike Owens, a famous Welsh International rugby player. He was tough-looking and his nose appeared to have been broken at some time. When he was angry he stuffed his hands in his pockets; rumour had it that he did this to avoid striking anyone who annoyed him. He appeared very casual, wearing his battledress like a workman's overall, but from the start it was obvious that he knew his job. He had two weeks to turn us into paratroopers and to him this was all that mattered. It was equally plain that he had never read any of those drill pamphlets which say that the best test of alertness is the way you salute flags on staff cars. He was quite oblivious to the finer points of foot drill and when he marched us away ran all his commands into one: 'Attention – left turn – quick march – right wheel!'

The first week at Ringway was devoted to teaching us how to exit properly from balloons and aircraft. For this purpose there was a hangar full of ingenious equipment, called 'Kilkenny's Circus', which was named after the wing commander who had thought it all up. The hangar housed the cut-down fuselage of a Whitley bomber, one of the first RAF aircraft which had been adapted to drop parachutists. The Whitley had a hole in the floor through which you dropped. There were slides similar to those found in children's playgrounds except for their being sawn off halfway down. You slid down these, assuming the correct landing position: feet and knees together, legs bent at the knee, back curved, head tucked in and arms bent to shield the face. You had to ensure that you landed on one side of your body and rolled with the force of the impact, which was said to be equal to the shock of jumping off a twelve-foot wall. It was considered dangerous to land with feet apart or to attempt a 'stand-up' landing. Coconut mats were placed beneath the equipment in the hangar for the trainees to land on.

Another device for landing practice was a wire which stretched from the roof down to an upright railway sleeper. You climbed up and slung a toggle rope and wheel over this wire, jumped off and hung on. You came down at a cracking pace watching the post getting larger and larger. At the command 'Go!' you released your grip and rolled into the correct landing position on the mat. Some trainees were mesmerised by the post in front of them or were too scared to let go. They slammed into it, and that was that.

There was also a simulated descent exercise, which involved climbing up to a platform in the hangar roof and putting on a parachute harness. A wire from this led up and over a wheel set high up in the roof and down to a winch. You stepped into space and a RAF NCO let you down a bit at a time. This gave a trainee experience in damping down the oscillation caused by the initial swing. One day a recruit stepped off when the winch was not secured. He plummeted sixty feet to land on his spine on the concrete floor. He screamed and writhed about in agony but was quickly whipped out of sight. No doubt the NCO whose carelessness caused this accident got into serious trouble.

Then there was the 'Fan'. This was a favourite with many trainees but it terrified me. You had to make your way through the supporting girders in the hangar roof to get to it. At one of the six descending positions you donned a harness which was fastened to a length of what looked like piano wire wound around a drum. These drums had a vaned fan at one end, hence the name, and when you jumped the fan was supposed to slow down your descent. By this time in Ringway's history thousands of men had used this equipment and as a result the fans were quite worn, one particularly so, the one I always ended up on. The NCOs preferred the Fan to any other piece of equipment because the shock of landing used to jolt all the loose change out of our pockets. They considered this a legitimate perk.

A tragic accident occurred while we were at Ringway. One of the RAF instructors was killed as a result of falling from an air-craft. He had omitted to secure himself properly when supervising the dispatch of trainees through the hole, a standard safety measure. On the back of each parachute was a strop with a clasp at one end which you secured to a wire running the whole length of the aircraft bulkhead. This was so that you could move down the aircraft when 'hooked up', as it was known. When you jumped the strop played out, the other end being attached to the bag enclosing your parachute. The bag pulled off and the parachute started to develop. A nylon tie secured the bag to the top of the parachute and this would break as you floated down to earth, thus releasing the strop. In practice the whole movement was almost instantaneous when leaving the plane. A stick of men having jumped, the strops were pulled back into the aircraft by the instructor to avoid their fouling the tail plane or undercarriage. Apparently this RAF instructor had been recovering the strops when the pilot suddenly increased speed. The unexpected movement and added slipstream caught him unawares and he was dragged through the hole, falling seven hundred feet to his death. Everyone was very upset over this as he was a popular NCO. He had done scores of jumps and had been at Ringway since parachuting began.

On the Saturday at the end of the first week we were taken up in a Whitley for air experience. This bomber was twin-engined, large and slow. When she hit an air pocket she would drop like a stone and then rise slowly again. The interior was claustrophobic. You had to sit with your back against one side of the aircraft with your knees drawn up. The only light was that which percolated through cracks in the fuselage or the hole in the floor. It is not difficult to imagine conditions in a dark hot interior only partially illuminated by glimmers of light, with the occupants half-choked by the smell of aircraft dope and high octane fuel, and deafened by the roar of the two huge engines as the old plane dipped and rose in the skies over Manchester. The pilot took evasive action to give us an idea of what it would be like if we met flak. Next we were invited to crawl along the fuselage and peer down through the hole. A strange thing happened with one of the volunteers, who came from the Westminster Dragoons. He became fascinated by what he saw and tried to crawl out, with the result that he had to be forcibly restrained. Apparently this fascination is a common phenomenon.

Later we were taken out to Tatton Park in Cheshire, where all the training jumps took place, to watch some trainees doing their first day-balloon jump. These balloons were old barrage balloons with a cage suspended underneath, the cage being constructed of light metal with canvas sides. A replica of the

Whitley hole dominated the floor of the cage and there was a bar overhead, to which the parachute strops were attached prior to jumping. The RAF instructor stood astride the hole to supervise each exit. There was only just room for the four terrified trainees in the corners of the cage. The balloon, which ascended to seven hundred feet, was paid out by a cable attached to a winch in the back of an RAF truck. When it halted the instructor shouted, 'Ready Number One.' The first victim swung his legs into the hole. There was a second's pause, then the instructor bellowed 'Go!' The trainee 'pushed off' correctly, snapping his arms down his sides and exiting through the hole at the position of 'attention'. It was a good exit and after a long drop we heard the crack of the parachute opening. Owing to the lack of slipstream, when a jump was made from a static balloon there was a drop of a hundred and fifty feet before the parachute developed. This is quite a distance—like falling off the top of a high cliff. When the parachute opened, there were still five hundred and fifty feet to go, which gave plenty of time to dampen down any oscillation or deal with any other emergency. Down they came one after another to the accompaniment of shouts of 'Go! Go! Go!' Ike Owens commented on each exit and told us what mistakes to avoid.

Suddenly there was trouble. One man's parachute had not opened and he kicked and screamed as he fell, frantically tugging at the lift webs of his harness. Down he hurtled with his parachute streaming behind him, but not in the familiar umbrella shape. We all thought we were witnessing a 'Roman Candle', the airborne term for a parachute which fails to develop. When it seemed almost certain he was doomed we heard a crack as his parachute opened, but the trainee knew nothing of this: he had fainted. Most of us must have looked rather green round the gills. However, Ike merely remarked, 'Damp chute – develops late – often happens.'

Not a tremor passed over his face, which reassured some of us, but others had already decided then and there that parachuting was not for them. No one thought any the worse of them for this as all of us have some fear that we cannot overcome. Until a trainee had completed the full parachute course of eight jumps he could refuse at any time. There was no coercion. However, once he was issued with the red beret and wings it was a different matter. Refusal to jump was then treated as refusal to obey an order, the punishment being fifty-six days' detention in the glasshouse and RTU (Returned to Unit) with 'Lack of moral fibre' scrawled across the offender's conduct-sheet in red ink, or so we were told. It was a subdued and thoughtful squad which returned to Ringway that night.

The next morning we were issued with a grey jump overall without sleeves, and the close-fitting airborne steel helmet with its shock-absorbing rubber lining and chin guard. We were also given a nylon tie each. It was the custom to attach this tie, which was a piece of nylon cord about a foot long, to the opening of the zip-fastener on our overall. Each time we did a jump we tied a knot in it, which may account for the famous Army phrase 'Get knotted!' We were then taken to draw chutes. There was just time for a last dash to the toilets before embussing for the drive to Tatton Park for our first jump.

If we were nervous already the RAF driver seemed bent on proving that his driving was more terrifying than any parachute jump, and he largely succeeded. None of us spoke a word throughout the journey. We just sat clutching our parachutes and trying not to think of what lay ahead. The bus bumped across the grass towards the grounded balloon. We got out and gathered around Ike, who gave us some last-minute instructions and reassurances. The first four were told to get into the cage. Ike climbed over the side and stood astride the central hole. The RAF winchman played with his gear levers and the balloon began to ascend. It went up quite quickly like a lift and then stopped almost directly overhead at seven hundred feet. A slight breeze angled the wire securing the balloon to the truck, which ensured that the descending jumpers did not foul it. At the shouted words of command a group of parachutists came hurtling down, some exiting better than others as Ike bawled his approval or disapproval from above.

Then it was our turn. Four of us climbed into the cage, which was constantly dragging along the ground as the breeze caught the balloon. Jack Jolliffe had the Number One position and I was Number Two. I thought, 'If he goes through with it, so will I.'

As the balloon rose rapidly we peeped out through the laced spaces between the canvas and steel frame. The earth and our comrades seemed very far away; it was another world. The cage shuddered to a halt. Good Lord! Were we there already? There was a second's pause and then Ike bellowed, 'Action stations Number One!' Jack swung his highly polished boots into the hole; they looked like twin black mirrors. A muscle in his face twitched. 'Go!' shouted Ike. Jack vanished while his strop slapped about. There was a crack and Jack was airborne. Ike recovered Jack's strop and shouted: 'Action stations Number Two!' I repeated Jack's performance. 'Go!'

For a split second my arms suspended me in the centre of the hole before I whipped them in to my sides, clutching the seams of my trousers. I was falling – falling – falling. One hundred and fifty feet is a long way to travel before anything happens. The only sound was the fluttering of my clothing in the momentum of my own slipstream. My body seemed to bend forward slightly so that I was facing the earth, which appeared to be spinning up to meet me. I felt a tug at my shoulders and I had the sensation that I was shooting upwards like a rocket. I looked up to see my fully developed parachute hanging over me like a protective canopy. I grasped the lift webs and tried out the elementary principles of steering we had been taught. How can one describe a parachute descent in words? It has to be experienced at first hand to have any reality. I felt like an eagle soaring through the sky.

There was no fear. That had vanished when the parachute opened. I wanted the experience to go on for ever. Paratroops say there are only two real thrills in life: they both last five seconds and one of them is parachuting. My god-like feelings of omnipotence were rudely shattered by an RAF officer who was shouting landing instructions at me through a loudhailer. I had dampened down nearly all the initial oscillation but was still surprised at the force of the landing. I rolled onto my back, and struck the quick release of the harness. I struggled out of it and then collapsed the chute.

That was the first one over. We clapped one another on the

back and crowded into a mobile canteen for a celebration cup of tea. I noticed how worked up everyone was, as though they had been given a drug or something. Then I thought about the two balloon and five aircraft jumps still to come. That quietened me down a bit. On the coach-ride back we were over-excited and full of talk. What a difference from the trip out!

The following day we had to do two jumps from balloons, one in the morning and one at night. Everyone said the night balloon was the best jump of the lot because you couldn't see anything. In the morning it was spitting with rain, with gusty winds. We looked over Ringway Airport towards a building with a tall chimney which was always smoking. If the smoke went up straight we would jump, but not if it was at right angles to the chimney top as the wind force was then considered too strong. The smoke was blowing all over the place and we expected the jump to be cancelled, but the order came, 'Draw chutes.'

There was another silent ride to Tatton Park. When we arrived it was still windy, and the balloon, already airborne, was careering all over the sky, almost lifting the rear of the winch truck off the ground. The decision was made to carry on, so the cage was brought down and we climbed in. The ascent was terrifying, with the cage rolling and rocking violently. When we halted we still appeared to be moving; it was almost as if we were in an airship instead of a static balloon. Ike shouted out the orders and Jack made a good exit. Now it was my turn, but I was so scared that, instead of pushing off in the correct manner, I just fell out. My parachute pack caught the edge of the hole behind me and I somersaulted into space. Ike roared after me, 'You bloody fool, you don't deserve to live!'

After an alarming drop the chute opened, but I found myself upside down with both feet caught up in the rigging lines. Although I had been terrified until the chute opened I was no longer afraid. We had been shown in a training film how to deal with just such an emergency. I reached up and disentangled each boot in turn, then fell the right way up. There was barely time to dampen down the considerable oscillation before I hit the deck. My terrible exit was overlooked because I had got out of the mess I had put myself in.

The night balloon drop really did turn out to be the best jump. We drove out to Tatton Park and made our way over to the balloon, which blotted out the stars. The wind had died away to a faint breeze as we clambered by torchlight into the cage and made our way aloft. You couldn't see the ground, the sky, or even each other, and you felt cut off from the world completely. There was no impression of height. We felt no fear at all and jumped well. The descent was a wonderful experience, rather like floating down through a world composed of black velvet. Only a soft breeze gave any impression of movement. Once again the tranquillity was shattered by the RAF officer with his loudhailer giving landing instructions. Landing could be tricky at night because there was a tendency to reach for the ground with your feet; this could lead to a serious accident. It was important to maintain the correct landing position and hope for the best. When the landing did occur it was so unexpected that it knocked the stuffing right out of you for a moment.

We were now ready to do our first Whitley aircraft jump. In the morning we were shown more films and given more advice; everything was gone over again and again. After lunch we paraded in front of the hangars and were counted off into 'sticks' of about eight men. The RAF used the same term for dropping men as for dropping bombs.

We were marched to the Whitley and given the order, 'Emplane.' We clambered in and sat facing one another in equal numbers on each side of the hole. The engines roared into life and we bumped and bucketed over the tarmac before finally turning into the wind at the head of the runway. There was a pause. Then the engines reached a crescendo of noise and we began to roll forward.

The flight from Tatton Park was of short duration and we soon received the command, 'Hook up.' We fastened the hooks on the end of our parachute strops to the wire running the length of the aircraft, securing it with a split pin provided for this purpose. I glanced at my comrades and was relieved to see that they all looked as scared as I felt. Directly above the hole was a panel with two small electric lights on it, one red and the other green. One of the RAF crewmen came back and advised us that we were approaching the Dropping Zone or DZ as it was called. 'OK. Close up,' shouted the RAF instructor. 'Action stations Number One.' The first man swung his legs into the hole. The green light shone. 'Go!' yelled the instructor, and the first man vanished. 'Go!' and Jack went. 'Go!' and I went.

The slipstream caught me as soon as I came out, but the parachute opened immediately and I swung on the end of the rigging lines like a pendulum. The roar of the aircraft was suddenly cut off and once again there was that wonderful feeling of soaring through the air. The rest of the stick were descending on either side equally spaced. It was what is called a 'tight' stick as we had all made good fast exits. Now we would land as a complete section instead of being scattered over miles of country-side.

After this first aircraft descent we all agreed that it was pre-ferable to a balloon jump, with its long drop before the para-chute opened. Now that we had four knots in our nylon ties we began to feel more confident, as half of the eight-jump course was completed. The next two descents were to be made with containers. These were heavy metal cylinders about six feet in length, and the parachutes they were attached to were usually brightly coloured, denoting that they carried arms, ammunition or folding motor cycles. The two containers were slung under the aircraft like bombs. Before jumping, the fifth man out of a stick of eight had to shout 'Container! Container! Container!' thus giving the crew time to release them. If he forgot to do so he might come down between the pair of them and be thumped accordingly. The containers were dispatched in the middle of the stick for easy availability on landing.

During one of the jumps an extraordinary thing happened. After landing near the lake in Tatton Park we were astonished to hear cries for help from the sky and on looking up we saw a trainee going up instead of descending. We stood there in open-mouthed wonder as our comrade, a small wiry signalman, got more and more worried about his situation. Apparently he had drifted into the rising thermal current from the lake and, owing to the size of the parachute and his being so light, it was taking him up. The instructor shouted to him not to panic, and to pull down hard on one side of his lift webs to spill air out of the chute. This he did and eventually succeeded in bringing himself down to earth. When we saw that he was safe it became an occasion for great merriment, but at the time it must have been a most frightening experience. After this he was weighted down for each jump.

The remaining two jumps had to be done with a kitbag attached to the left leg. This was a new idea, the intention being that each paratrooper would land with his own weapons and ammunition and not have to run to a container upon which the enemy had already zeroed in with rifle or machine-gun fire. A kitbag, when full, weighed about seventy pounds and was secured to the leg with a quick-release gear. After jumping you pulled a pin which released the kitbag from your leg. It could then be lowered by a rope attached to your waist to a position about twenty feet beneath you. Kitbag descents were rapid because of the extra weight, but when the kitbag hit the ground directly beneath you your parachute 'breathed' and then let you down quite lightly, so this was a great improvement.

I received quite a scare on my second kitbag jump, for when my parachute opened and I looked down to release the kitbag I found to my horror that I was exactly over the centre of the lake. Although I had done river crossings I had never learned to swim, and it looked as though I was about to receive my first lesson. Down below I could see figures scurrying to a boat and beginning to row out to my rescue. However, I had no intention of getting even my feet wet if it could be humanly avoided, so, gauging the wind direction, I pulled down the lift webs so that the parachute canopy acted as a sail. I was descending faster than I can write these lines and the water came rushing up to meet me, but I held on and left the rest to God. The kitbag splashed into the lake as I rolled onto the bank with a yard to spare. I was lucky. Thankfully I made for the canteen and a quick cuppa.

Well, we had made it. Out of an original contingent of 165 men about 60 of us had completed the course and were now paratroopers.

On the Friday morning there was the official parade and we

were issued with our para wings, red berets and Parachute
Regiment cap badges. We removed our motley collection of
headgear and donned our red berets for the first time. It was
one of the greatest moments of our lives and one of the proudest.

The next day we proceeded on fourteen days' leave, which
counted as our embarkation leave now that we were qualified
parachutists. Upon our return we would be liable for overseas
service immediately.

At the end of our leave we had to report to Clay Cross, the
Airborne Forces Depot near Chesterfield. Here we were taught
battle drill. We were also given special lectures and shown training films. There was some bull but it was nothing like as bad as
in the RA. We did, however, have to blanco our equipment for
guards, even our para steel helmets. The training followed much
the same pattern as at Hardwick Hall, only there was more
emphasis on drill. The NCOs had a difficult task as we hailed
from every regiment and corps in the British Army, many
having their own interpretations of the Drill Book and rate of
marching. However, what we lacked in finish we made up for
in enthusiasm.

We were told we were going to a place in Wiltshire called
Keevil to do Stirling jumps. The Stirling was a four-engined
bomber recently adapted for towing gliders and dropping
parachutists. It proved a terrifying aircraft to jump from. It was
large, so large that we could easily stand upright in it to jump.
The hole in the floor was an enormous-looking rectangle about
six feet by four feet. When you stood on the lip awaiting the
green light signal to jump you could see a large area of the
ground below and a huge U-shaped bar, which was lowered for
the strops of the parachutes to go under so that they didn't foul
the tailplane.

Before we arrived one of the Stirling planes had dropped a
stick of men on some high-tension overhead cables; another
Stirling had landed amongst a squad of paras who were being
drilled on the main runway by an idiot NCO. Casualties had
occurred both times and we were told that the particular pilots
were training for D-Day. None of us was very happy, and on the
morning of our first jump we had another unnerving experience.

A Stirling was roaring down the runway to take off when one of its undercarriages collapsed. It careered round in circles, two of its airscrews chewing up the airfield. Luckily it did not catch fire but came to a halt in a great cloud of dust and smoke. The hapless paras inside were dragged out and staggered about drunkenly, but they were pushed on to another Stirling which took off immediately. This was done to prevent them losing their nerve.

Our first Stirling jump was not good. We took off and headed for Salisbury Plain. The RAF crewmen were not used to para-troops and thought we were all raving mad. Being six feet tall, I discovered that by standing up and jamming my steel helmet against some rods running along the roof of the aircraft I need not hold on to anything. We were approaching the DZ when an agitated crew member came up to me and said, 'Get your head away from those rods, Lofty, we can't turn the aircraft.' I was jamming the rudder controls. We had to go round once more and then one of the paras wouldn't jump, so round we went yet again and still he refused. We did another circle and he still wouldn't go, so that was that. He was unhooked, taken to the rear of the aircraft and made to sit down. The poor chap didn't need much persuasion as he was white-faced and trembling and was clinging to a large pipe for dear life. An NCO had to stay with him, as it had been known for a man left on his own and unhooked to follow his mates out of the plane when he saw them leave. The NCO tried to comfort him. It was difficult to meet his gaze, he was in such a state. He was a good-looking lad, definitely officer material, but this was the end of the road for him: all he could look forward to was fifty-six days' detention and being sent back to his unit with 'Lack of moral fibre' on his conduct-sheet.

We shuffled along behind one another. There was a small chap in front, then George Howard (a fellow Brightonian) and then me. When the small man jumped his helmet appeared to shave the lowered U-bar. I gulped. George went and I followed him. I shut my eyes, fearing instant decapitation. I felt a tre-mendous blow like a rabbit punch in the back of my neck, which was due to the four-engined slipstream from this ugly aircraft. The initial oscillation was terrific and it proved impossible to dampen it down to any great extent. Jack Jolliffe, who followed me out, said that he too had noticed that our heads just seemed to scrape under the U-bar. Anyway, no one actually lost his head but several lost their nerve and refused to jump any more. One man screamed as he jumped, which really put the wind up me.

The next jump was aborted because a Polish paratrooper had had a Roman Candle and was splattered all over the runway. Apparently they didn't want us to be 'put off'. This was one of the few times when I actually landed in an aircraft.

I had an equally disturbing experience a few days later. A bus-load of girls had been brought to the DZ as a treat to watch us jump. They were on some sort of war work and when I emerged from the Stirling one of them screamed. I nearly passed out, as I thought my parachute hadn't opened. I hit the ground heavily and heard moaning. It was George Howard being dragged along by his parachute and obviously in agony. I sprinted over, collapsed his chute and got him out of his harness. He was clutching one of his arms, which he had apparently hit on the U-bar when he was exiting. This meant that I had to roll up two parachutes and somehow get George to an ambulance. A small boy appeared, anxious to help, and I gave him sixpence to carry George's parachute about half a mile to the truck. The parachute bundle was nearly as big as he was, but he staggered manfully alongside me as I carried my own chute under one arm, supporting George with the other.

We had nearly reached the truck when a high-ranking RAF officer approached. I was never very well up on RAF ranks, but he had 'scrambled egg' all over his cap and rings halfway up his arm. He was furious that I had allowed the small boy to carry George's parachute, and started leading off about it. There was I with a parachute under one arm and holding up George with the other. I was convinced George had broken his arm and I gave this senior officer a right mouthful of abuse. Obviously no one had ever spoken to him like that before and he appeared about to have a fit when, luckily for me, an airborne officer rescued me from a dire fate.

The first week at Keevil was a bad one for the airborne forces. More than a hundred qualified paratroopers refused to jump from Stirlings and were placed under close arrest prior to court martial and the punishment already mentioned. The guard room was absolutely jam-packed with these victims of the Stirling.

So it was a much reduced and chastened contingent which returned to Clay Cross. George Howard and I volunteered for the Independent Parachute Company, which specialised in small-scale operations. The way we had developed our airborne forces I didn't fancy being in a battalion or divisional drop, and I always thought that the smaller the operation the greater the chance of success. George was accepted but I was not considered suitable for some reason. His parting words to me were, 'Remember, if ever you want to see me after the war, go into The Volunteer in Brighton, and you'll find me lying across the bar dead drunk.' Funnily enough, I happened to pass The Volunteer one day in 1945 and went in merely with the idea of having a drink to George's memory. There he was lying across the bar completely blotto.

That week we received our postings to active service battalions. An Ox and Bucks lad and myself went to the 2nd Battalion of the Parachute Regiment. 'You're going to a good mob,' said the sergeant. We arrived at our new unit just after my nineteenth birthday and found ourselves standing in the court-yard of a very fine old building called Stoke Rochford Hall. It was situated near a hamlet of the same name not far from Grantham in Lincolnshire. It had once been the home of Sir Isaac Newton, who propounded the law of gravity, so it was an apt place to house paratroopers. We were greeted by a signals sergeant with these words: 'Gentlemen, you are joining a battalion living on its past glories.' Of course the battalion already had a splendid war record and had seen a great deal of action. The commanding officer was Lieutenant-Colonel John Frost, a living legend in airborne forces, having led the highly successful Bruneval raid on a German radar station in occupied France in 1942. Since leading that raid he had commanded the battalion in North Africa, Sicily and Italy, collecting a DSO and MC *en route*. However, with D-Day approaching, the sergeant's remarks seemed pessimistic to say the least.

That afternoon we paraded in two ranks in front of the Hall for the colonel's inspection. He asked me what unit I had previously served with and when he learnt I was ex-Artillery asked, 'How would you like to serve in our Mortar Platoon?' As he seemed to think I would be happy there I agreed. The Ox and Bucks lad ended up in the Heavy Machine Gun Platoon. We were both in 'S' Company, which meant 'Support'. I liked the sound of this as it implied that someone else would be in front.

We were allocated rooms right at the top of the Hall in what at one time would have been the servants' quarters. The entire ceiling of our room was covered with pin-up pictures of Betty Grable. In those days the Army did not permit nudes on the walls. Our pin-ups were very chaste. Miss Grable's pictures were mostly head and shoulders or showed her in a one-piece bathing suit or tights. Even mothers and clergymen couldn't have objected to them.

There was only one other occupant of the room when I entered. He was built like a tank and was fair-haired and blue-eyed and, I was glad to discover, friendly. As we had the rest of the day off I sat down on my kitbag to write a letter to my girl in Brighton. The sound of a fuse fizzing between my legs sent me hurtling into the air. 'Slapsie', for that was his nickname, roared with laughter at the success of the first of many such jokes he was to play on me. He was from the East End and we hit it off straight away. He always called me 'Kid', just one of the various nicknames I was to be given in the Army.

When the other occupants came in at teatime I was given the full treatment. 'Stand up, let's have a look at you, young soldier.' I stood up. 'Christ! What's this?' asked one of them in mock horror. He had discovered the carefully cut pieces of plywood which squared off my large and small packs and pouches, relics of my 'bull' days with the artillery. My beautiful bits of plywood quickly became matchwood under a great Geordie heel. A Scot produced a razor blade. 'You're improperly dressed,' he said and whipped off my bought Parachute Regiment shoulder flashes and Pegasus divisional signs and handed them to me. In the

2nd Battalion we wore only the issue flashes, which were drab in comparison. I was also wearing on each arm flashes with 'Airborne' on them, which made these terrible men hoot with laughter, as only glider-borne troops were entitled to this particular flash.

They laughed at my discomfiture but suddenly one of them said, 'Here, put this on.' He handed me a beautiful gold lanyard, obviously made out of parachute nylon rigging line, the removal of which was a court martial offence. This gold lanyard was worn only by the 2nd Battalion and was produced as follows. After a jump a para would cut off a rigging line and secrete it about his person. Back at camp he would persuade someone skilled in the art to plait it into a lanyard. He would then dissolve a mepacrine tablet in a saucer of water in which he would place the lanyard, leaving it overnight. In the morning he would have a beautiful gold lanyard. No one could recall the genius who first devised this unauthorised use of medical supplies, which was based on the idea that if these tablets could turn a man yellow they would do the same for nylon. Because of this practice the 2nd Battalion were known in the First Para Brigade as the Mepacrine Chasers. The 1st Battalion had dark green lanyards and the 3rd red. Everyone in our battalion had a 'larny' lanyard, as it was known, and it was very highly regarded. Wearing this spectacular gold lanyard, whitening the parachute badge on your right shoulder and touching up the mortar badge with red ink was not bull but personal pride. According to our lads there was a subtle difference between the two.

It was now May, the weather was warm, and we were out all day and often all night training. A typical day commenced with reveille blown on the bugle, but sometimes on the bagpipes, as our battalion had a strong Scots flavour, a number of the officers and men having previously served with the Cameronians. We paraded outside Stoke Hall in shorts and singlets and, led by the colonel, went for a mile run before breakfast. Our meals were served in huge tents erected where the tennis courts had been. The food was good and plentiful and there were enormous tins of jam on each table. At eight we paraded for weapon inspection.

As long as a para was washed, shaved and tidy no one bothered, but personal weapons had to be spotless and punishments were severe for just a speck of dust on a foresight.

We then changed into the appropriate dress for the morning's training and from half-past eight to ten we practised mortar drill with our 3-inch mortars. This weapon consisted of three parts, the barrel, legs and base plate, each weighing roughly forty pounds. It was a simple but highly effective piece to use and the British mortar bombs had a devastating effect on explosion. There was some sort of chemical propellant which could be attached to the fins of each bomb so as to increase the range. In action the barrel, legs and base plate were carried by three separate men and the remainder of the section carried six ten-pound mortar bombs. Our section sergeant, Maurice Kalikoff, was an exacting instructor whose aim was speed and accuracy, and we practised over and over again until he was reasonably satisfied with our performance.

Maurice was a Russian Jew. He had been born in Kiev and his family had fled from Russia during a pogrom. He still retained the Slav's sad, almost fatalistic, outlook on life and was quietly spoken – for a sergeant. He was a first-class soldier and one of the finest human beings I have ever met.

We had a mid-morning tea break of about twenty minutes and resumed training from ten-thirty to noon when we had lunch, which lasted for about an hour and a quarter, giving us a chance of a snooze. In the afternoon there would be yet more weapon training or camouflage and gas lectures, sometimes illustrated with films. Unless we had a night exercise we finished at 4 pm and had tea.

We were also shown propaganda films and given lectures which were designed to clarify what we were fighting for. Getting the English worked up enough to defend democracy was an uphill task, as the average soldier appeared to have only three basic interests: football, beer and crumpet. In the paras the order was reversed. Few of my comrades seemed to take anything seriously, but their weapon expertise was obvious. For Jerry, our German enemy, they had a half-admiring, half-contemptuous attitude.

Our ideals could be summed up as a willingness to fight any-one at any time, a determination not to let down our officers and comrades, and a resolve to uphold the formidable reputation of the Parachute Regiment.

On some of the night exercises we were driven in a sealed truck round the flat Lincolnshire countryside and then flung out in groups of three with a map and a compass. In a blacked-out Britain and with such a featureless landscape, not unlike Hol-land, it was very difficult to discover just where you were. They dropped us off at about 10 pm and it was entirely up to each team how to get back to Stoke Hall and so to bed. If you were dropped with two keen types your luck was out because they would spend about an hour trying to find a landmark; having found one a route had to be worked out, compass bearings taken and so on. If you were with two old soldiers they would wait until a local farmer came staggering home from the pub, then one of them would hoist him off his feet while the other growled, 'Where are we, mate? Which is the way to Stoke Rochford?' Upon being told, they would lower the farmer to his heels, glance at the map, then say 'Righto, this way!' Within half an hour they would be back in bed. With more conscientious com-panions you might blunder round Lincolnshire until dawn.

I was with such a pair one night when we came to a large stretch of concrete. 'This is it, the Great North Road,' said the leader, 'and that's Grantham down there.' 'It doesn't look like a road to me,' I said, 'and you wouldn't see all those lights in Grantham with the blackout.' 'Shut up, young soldier,' I was told, 'now we'll just nip across.' We fell flat on the deck as an American Flying Fortress took off over us. We were standing on the edge of a runway.

On another occasion when I was out with two keen types we came to a cutting through which ran the main railway line to London. We had to get across this line somehow. Gingerly we made our way down one side of the cutting and stood absolutely still listening. There wasn't a sound, but the leader crept for-ward and laid his ear to one of the railway lines. He had seen an Indian do this in an old Western to detect the approach of the 'Iron Horse'. 'It's OK, there's nothing coming,' he said. We only just got across the tracks and flattened ourselves against the other side of the cutting as an express thundered through. It was a shattering experience.

It was now nearly into June and getting really warm, but we never let up in our training. We proceeded on a Field Firing Exercise over the Derbyshire hills, firing live ammunition. We marched sixty miles in three days. Most of the time it rained. One evening we arrived at Glossop and were billeted in a church hall. The next day we marched into the surrounding hills and our platoon officer, Lieutenant Woods, gave a demonstration of how to blow an instant mortar pit with explosives. He was a tall slim man, rather quiet but very efficient and cool under fire according to the veterans of the platoon who had seen action with him in Sicily.

One thing we youngsters quickly learned on these exercises was the airborne 'mucking-in' spirit. No matter how tired you felt you never sat back and let your comrades do all the work but pitched in without being told. The best example of this spirit was given by the officers and NCOs who, even after a long and arduous march, never sat down until we all had a hot meal inside us and were bedded down for the night. I often saw Lieutenant Woods, who was not a big man despite his height, refuse to sit down or even have a mouthful of tea until we were all seen to. Naturally the men responded to such positive treatment, but for all this discipline was strict. We could not address officers except through a senior NCO, and yet they would often talk to you about your home and post-war ambitions. They knew all our strengths and weaknesses.

Of course the majority of officers and NCOs had already proved themselves in action, and we new boys wondered how we would behave when the bullets started flying.

On 5 June 1944 I was on guard with Gerry, a para from Liverpool; all night long we heard the throb of aircraft engines. The next day we were taken to the RAF Regiment camp at Grantham to try out their battle course and to test our new gas masks which had just been issued. At 11 am we heard cheering and we were told that it was D-Day and that Allied troops had landed in Normandy. The seaborne landings had been preceded by an airborne attack by our rivals, the 6th Airborne Division. When our lads discovered this they rioted and were only pacified when our officers assured them that they had been kept back for 'something special'. Personally I felt relieved that we had not gone but this relief was not shared by most of my comrades, who thought that the 1st Airborne should have played a part in D-Day rather than the 6th, whom we regarded as amateurs.

After D-Day, as the Allies swept forward across France, we stood to for one operation after another. We seemed to be ever-lastingly round the sand-table being briefed. On one such occasion I was selected for a guard of honour for General 'Boy' Browning, GOC Airborne Forces. We had to practise a spot of ceremonial drill for his arrival. We saw his car approaching at speed and presented arms in the general salute, only to be showered with stones and dust as his car did a U-turn in front of us. He leaned out and shouted to the colonel, and then he was gone.

About this time Joe Hamilton, a very smart and keen young soldier, was promoted sergeant and we went on yet another exercise. At one point an airborne brigadier stood up in his staff car to watch us pass. We were all-in, but still going. When Joe saw the brigadier he straightened up and the brigadier, noticing him, said, 'How goes it, sergeant?' 'Fine, sir, fine,' replied Joe. A great shout came from the paratroopers following him – 'Blackleg!' Even the brigadier laughed.

August came and our jeeps were replaced by Bren gun carriers. We had two, driven by George Hines, another Brigh-tonian, and 'Chalky' White, a Londoner. Our platoon was moved from Stoke Hall because the tracks tore up the drive. We were put in Nissen huts with 'C' Company on the edge of an aerodrome and much nearer to Grantham. The training became more intense, with 'long carries', which meant sixty pounds of mortar equipment or bombs on a march, as well as battle order. It was very hot and I seemed to be constantly sweating.

Slapsie was given a job as ammunition storeman. Being a handy sort of chap he decided to make himself a cigarette lighter, which was not unusual, as factory workers producing Spitfires also did this sort of thing. However Slapsie made his to fit into the nose of one of our ten-pound mortar bombs. He removed the detonator and replaced it with an identical screw-cap fitting containing his lighter. The doctored bomb was then placed back on the racks alongside its more deadly companions. Occasionally someone who dropped into the Arms Store for a chat would forget themselves, pull out a cigarette and ask for a light. Viewing his victim with withering scorn Slapsie would shout, 'This is an ammo store, not a bloody canteen! All right – here.' He would then offer the smoker a lighted ten-pound mortar bomb. The look on the smoker's face had to be seen to be appreciated.

Despite his escapades Slapsie was a very popular member of the platoon, though most of us preferred to hear about his jokes rather than participate in them for there always had to be a victim. I remember waking up one morning to find my only pair of boots laced neatly together and filled to the brim with beer, at least I like to think it was beer. 'Good for your feet, Kid,' said a grinning Slapsie.

One day we were taken to Stoke Hall for a briefing and once more sat round the sand-table. This time the briefing concerned a place called Arnhem in Holland. None of us had ever heard of it. Our battalion was to land outside the town and secure the DZ. One company alone was expected to capture and hold a large road bridge in the centre of the town. As this place was over sixty miles behind the enemy lines, the task seemed impossible for one battalion, and the men said so in no uncertain manner. We were told not to talk about this operation, as it was touch and go if it was on. I don't believe we even stood to on this occasion. We all thought it had fallen through but kept our mouths shut anyway.

We stood to yet again for a sort of beefed-up Arnhem operation, code-named Market Garden. On this occasion the whole of the 1st Airborne Division was to drop at Arnhem, with the 2nd Battalion being given the important task of securing the main road bridge in the centre of the town. Montgomery intended to thrust a spear of Allied airborne troops deep into enemy-held territory in Holland and we were to be at the very tip of this spearhead. The plan was for the American 101st and

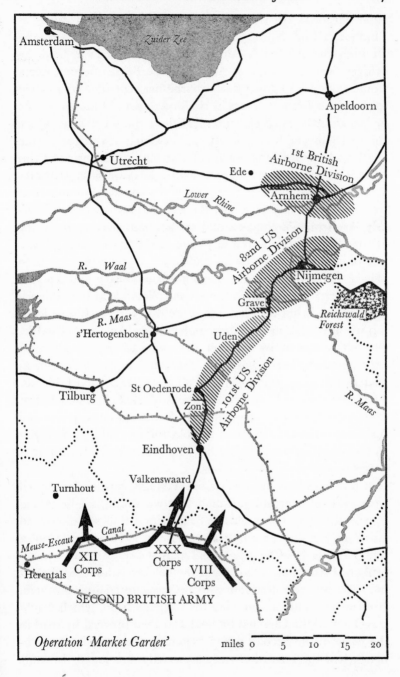

Operation 'Market Garden'

82nd Airborne Divisions to seize canal and river crossings at
Eindhoven and Nijmegen and for the British 1st Airborne
Division and the Polish Para Brigade to capture and hold the
bridges over the Rhine at Arnhem. The British Second Army
would then sweep down this airborne-held corridor completely
splitting the German forces in Holland in two, at the same time
outflanking the northern end of Hitler's Siegfried Line. Once
this was achieved Montgomery could swing eastwards across the
heathlands of Germany towards Berlin, ending the war in 1944.

This operation was not greeted with the enthusiasm that previous plans had aroused because it was fairly clear to all that it
was going to be a dicey affair. We were to land seven miles outside Arnhem. Intelligence told us we had nothing to worry
about. There was no armour in the area and only second-rate
line-of-communication troops and Luftwaffe personnel – a piece
of cake, in fact. We wondered about this as we sat and listened to
the briefing, but at least in the Second World War the ordinary
soldier knew what the plan was and our general would be leading us, not stuck in a chateau miles behind the line of battle.
We felt reassured by the fact that we had one of the most
experienced airborne battalion commanders in the world, as
well as an outstanding platoon officer in Lieutenant Woods.
The latter showed little emotion about Market Garden, whereas
Platoon Sergeant Jackman was full of enthusiasm. I questioned
this show of confidence but the old soldiers said, 'Don't you
worry, cowboy, he's the kiddie.' Translated, this meant that
Sergeant Jackman was first-class.

A few days later 'Brum' Davis, 'Young Geordie' and myself
were told by Sergeant Jackman that we would not be taking
part in the operation after all. Brum was a thickset, dark-eyed
lad from Birmingham; he was cheerfully aggressive but not a
bully. Young Geordie, whose real name I cannot recall, was an
orphan. Lieutenant Woods said the colonel considered that at
nineteen we were too young to be parachuted into Arnhem.
Instead we would accompany the baggage train, which would
travel across the Channel by boat and then proceed by road in
the wake of the Second Army, rejoining the battalion at Arnhem when the operation was successfully concluded. In some

ways I was not sorry, for now that the time for action was imminent I did not feel as confident as I would have liked to. I cannot speak for my companions, but for me the news was a mixture of relief and disappointment. The 6-pounder anti-tank guns were not being sent either, as the sights and necessary spares had not arrived.

The operation was to commence on Sunday 17 September 1944. Although the three of us were to be left behind we still took part in normal platoon activities. The last days were spent in checking all stores and equipment and in section briefing. Sergeant Hamilton warned us that if we refused to jump in action we would be shot. Sergeant Kalikoff became obsessed with our proposed method of exit from the aircraft and we had to hobble through a Nissen hut with a fully loaded kitbag on one leg practising jumping and keeping close together. It was baking hot in the Nissen hut but Maurice was determined that we should keep a tight stick and all land together. As we hobbled through the huts we cursed him, under our breath, but no doubt this last-minute drill did the trick.

Slapsie did his best to keep our morale up by subjecting all of us to his particular brand of practical joke. We were sitting on our beds one lunchtime when a cat wandered into the hut. There are always stray cats and dogs around Army camps, well-fed and petted by the men. This cat, which had grown over-confident, approached Slapsie's bed. A huge hand seized it behind the neck and Slapsie got up, tucking the cat under his left arm so that its head was facing to his rear. He held its back legs with his left hand and its tail in his right. We looked on in amazement as he strolled to the top of the hut with the frantically struggling moggie firmly pinned against his left side. He turned and made the announcement, 'Bagpipes,' then marched down the hut, biting the cat's tail at intervals. Our eyes goggled as the cat screeched at every bite, producing a sound not unlike a hideous parody of the Scots' national instrument. Reactions to this were mixed. Some brave souls tried to rescue the cat and were knocked over two beds for their pains, others threatened to report Slapsie to the RSPCA, but most of us were helpless with laughter.

On the Friday morning we were taken in sealed trucks to one of Grantham's cinemas to see a film. Airborne Military Police lined the path on both sides of us. The film was called 'Hellzapoppin' with Olsen and Johnson, two zany American comedians. I thought it was the funniest film I'd ever seen in my life.

We spent the next twenty-four hours getting our equipment ready, loading the vehicles and writing that last letter, which would not be posted until we had left Grantham. Three old soldiers were missing: having decided that Arnhem was just one more abortive operation, they had disappeared in the fleshpots of Nottingham. The provost jeeps toured likely areas in an effort to find them, but in vain. Brum, Young Geordie and myself were warned to get ready. As we had not been in the battalion long, we were designated as bomb carriers and were given the harness with six ten-pound mortar-bombs to cart into action. We were issued with Dutch occupation money, maps, escape saws, forty rounds of .303 rifle ammo, two .36 grenades, an anti-tank grenade, a phosphorus bomb, and a pick and shovel, as well as the rifles we already had.

On the Saturday night most of us relaxed; some played football, others darts. Some read and some wrote letters. I went over to the canteen and sat on a chair with my feet up on the unlit stove. The bagpiped cat crept on to my lap and purred contentedly as I scratched its ear. One of the 'C' Company men showed me a religious tract he had just received in a parcel from home. On it was a picture of a windmill and the words 'Lost on the Zuider Zee'. He thought it was a bad omen; it was certainly a strange coincidence.

I was busy trying to reassure him when Slapsie walked in. As he passed me he hit me playfully on the shoulder with the heel of his hand. I shot over backwards, the chair, cat and myself going in different directions. 'Cup of tea, Kid?' he asked. He fetched two teas and some wads and we sat there in silence, the old veteran of Narvik, North Africa, Sicily and Italy, and the young and untried soldier. Only two years before I had been in the Army Cadet Corps. As I recall we didn't talk much except that Slapsie thought there was no problem. 'Be back here in a fortnight and down at The Black Dog again,' was how he summed up. We eventually turned in and I slept surprisingly well.

Sunday started off just like any other day except for some butterflies in the stomach. 'Have a good breakfast,' they advised, 'as you don't know when you'll get your next meal.'

Only one of our Bren gun carriers was needed and George Hines and Chalky tossed up for the privilege of driving it. George won and elected to go, so Chalky travelled with the baggage party. The transport arrived to take us to Folkingham aerodrome where the Douglas C47 Dakotas were waiting to lift us to Arnhem. These planes belonged to the Ninth US Air Force; they were drawn up *en masse* and looked very impressive. Someone dished out great mugs of tea and bacon sandwiches, and a camera crew on a truck came along and filmed us. We jumped about and waved our mugs in the air. The excitement was beginning to build up, everyone was laughing and shouting; the atmosphere had suddenly become like a school outing or picnic. All our doubts seemed to be swept away in a sudden surge of confidence. At last we were going and we somehow knew that this time there would be no stand-down.

Chapter 2

AIRBORNE TO ARNHEM

WE CLAMBERED aboard the aircraft on the order 'Emplane.'
The twin engines burst into life with a shattering roar, the plane
gave a shudder and rolled forward along the tarmac. The
American pilots taxied in Vic formation. Our aircraft lurched
over as it turned at the head of the runway and stopped.
Staggered on either side of us were two other aircraft and behind
us were three more.

The plane shook as the engine revolutions increased. We
began to pick up speed and were soon thundering along the
runway. The noise grew to a howling storm of sound as we
bumped and bucketed along. We glued our faces to the small
windows and waved to our comrades in the other aircraft. It
seemed as though we would hurtle on until we smashed into the
boundary fence but a subtle change in the motion of the aircraft
told us we were airborne; Lieutenant Woods confirmed this by
lifting his outstretched hands and smiling. It was approxi-
mately 11.30 am and – a sobering thought – we would be in
Holland before lunch was over.

It suddenly struck me how much danger I was in. Here I was
in this slow fragile aircraft (hadn't I already seen two blow up?)
and we might well meet flak or enemy fighters. I wondered what
the German reception committee was preparing for us. Cannon
fire? Machine guns? Tanks? Cold steel? 'What the hell am I
doing here?' I asked myself. 'I must be bloody mad!' However,
a glance round the interior of the aircraft somewhat reassured
me when I saw how cool and cheerful my comrades were.

We watched the friendly soil of England drop away as we
rose ponderously heavenwards. The Dakota was a sluggish aircraft and completely unarmed. When our aerial armada reached

the coast we fell in with our fighter escort, mostly RAF Hawkers, Tempests and Typhoons armed with cannons and rockets. We had been promised 'maximum fighter support', which meant a thousand aircraft and was very comforting.

The imposing airborne army swung out over the North Sea and we settled down for the journey. We sat eight-a-side down the round ribbed fuselage on bench-type seats. We were a right British cocktail of mixed blood: English, Irish, Scots and Welsh; Geordies, Scouses, Cockneys, men like Brum from the Midlands, men from Cambridge, Kent and Sussex. There were three Brightonians in our platoon. Some of us had been shop assistants, others salesmen, farmers, and barrow boys; there was even a poacher.

Lieutenant Woods as Number One was seated next to the open doorway. I was Number Fifteen and the man behind me, the last man out, was Maurice Kalikoff. I recalled all the tales the old soldiers had told me about Jerry: the relative merits of panzer grenadiers and our opposite numbers, the Green Devils of the formidable German Parachute Army; the Tiger tanks with tracks a yard wide and reputed to weigh nearly seventy tons; the 88mm dual-purpose gun; the MG34 heavy machine gun with its zip-fastener rate of fire; the famous Schmeisser sub-machine gun whose 9mm ammo could also be used in our poor imitation, the Sten gun. By comparison the Schmeisser was a precision job.

I tried to tell myself that this was what I had always wanted. It went with the red beret, wings and jump pay. We were flying at about four thousand feet over masses of billowing cloud which reflected the sunshine and made me think I was already in heaven. It was one of those moments in life of sheer beauty. The Dakota droned on over the sea. Talking was impossible so we either dozed or read. I had a copy of the *Reader's Digest*, which contained a story of how a rescue team searching for a crashed aircraft in a remote part of China had found a page from a *Digest* stuck to one of the wings of the wrecked plane. This story illustrated in graphic fashion how these handy little magazines often turned up in the most surprising places.

We were nearing the Dutch coast and were warned to brace

ourselves as the aircraft dived down through the clouds to about two thousand feet. We were still over the North Sea when a German naval vessel opened fire at us. Fortunately it was a small boat and only had a machine gun. The American pilot took instant evasive action and we held on to one another, bracing our feet as we banked alarmingly. We watched fascinated as a stream of tracer bullets arched towards us, slowly at first but then finally whipping past the open doorway like angry hornets. Some of our fighter escort peeled off and swept down to the attack; the German vessel vanished in a storm of rocket fire. We were undamaged and quickly resumed our position in the armada. Quite a number of us had to make use of the brown paper bags issued for sickness. Fancy giving people bacon sand-wiches before take-off!

Now we were told that the Dutch coastline lay just ahead, and my stomach did another somersault. All that marked the coastline of flooded Holland was a long ridge of land, not unlike the spine of some extinct prehistoric reptile. As we flew inland the water gradually gave way to ribbons of soil and then whole fields. We were very relieved at this as few of us had any faith in the issue life jackets, especially with the amount of kit we were carrying. Looking out of the windows we could see that the RAF had marked the trail to Arnhem with one blazing flak tower after another.

An American crewman came back and told us we were going down to seven hundred feet for the run-in. We put on our close-fitting helmets and adjusted our rubber chin guards. We hooked up and then heaved the kitbags containing six mortar bombs, pick, shovel, rifle and small pack on to our legs, securing them with special web straps. As each of us had at least a hundred pounds of equipment we would be sure of a rapid descent and little oscillation, and would be a difficult target for enemy machine gunners. We stood upright and closed up behind one another in single file. Our right hand held the kitbag grip and our left was on the shoulder of the man in front. Someone cracked, 'Pass right down the car, please!' Another joker plucked at my parachute and said, 'Blimey, cowboy, this isn't a chute, it's an old army blanket.'

The author (left) in 1943, shortly before he joined the Parachute Regiment, photographed in Brighton with a friend, Bill Gregory HU 2880

Trainee parachutists making balloon descents at Tatton Park, Manchester HU 28877

'Kilkenny's Circus': recruits being shown how to fall and roll correctly at the Parachute Training School, Ringway, Manchester   H 22872

Men of the 1st Parachute Brigade (which included the author's battalion) boarding a Dakota, 17 September 1944   K 7588

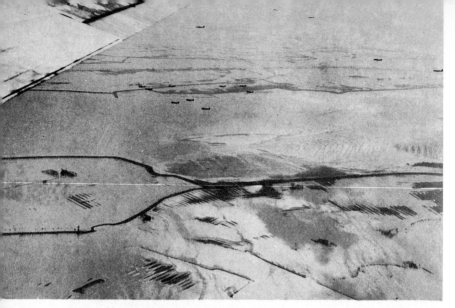

View of the flooded Dutch landcape. This photograph was taken by one of the fighters escorting the gliders and troop transports of the First Allied Airborne Army   PL 37777

Descent of the 1st Parachute Brigade at Renkum Heath, six miles southwest of Arnhem, 17 September 1944: a still from a piece of film shot by an official cameraman   MH 22710

It was essential that we followed the man in front out quickly as any hesitation could mean we would be hopelessly scattered on the DZ. Lieutenant Woods stood framed in the doorway, the slipstream plucking impatiently at the scrim netting on his helmet. The red light glowed steadily and then the green light winked on. 'Go!' The lieutenant vanished. We shuffled along the heaving deck of the Dakota . . . three . . . four . . . five . . . an American crewman had set up a cine camera and was filming our exit . . . six . . . seven . . . eight . . . a chap from Maidstone half turned and shouted something with a grin but it was lost in the roar of the engines . . . nine . . . ten . . . eleven . . . through the doorway I could see a huge Hamilcar glider on tow right alongside us; one wing of it was on fire but the glider pilot gave us the thumbs-up sign . . . twelve . . . thirteen . . . fourteen . . . the man in front of me hunched over slightly as he went out. Almost before his helmet disappeared I jumped but the slipstream caught me and whirled me around, winding up my rigging lines. I was forced to let go of my kitbag grip in an effort to try and stop the winding up process, for if it reached the canopy I was finished. The roar of the aircraft engines had been cut off and for the first time since leaving England I could distinguish other sounds. All around me parachutists were being disgorged from Dakotas and I found myself in the middle of a blizzard of silk. The parachutes were all the colours of the rainbow; it was an unforgettable sight. I was conscious of taking part in one of the greatest airborne descents in the history of warfare but this exhilaration was tempered by the trouble I was in. Luckily the twisting rigging lines had reversed their motion and I spun beneath them as they unwound. I did not feel much like an eagle as I fell – the experience was more like being hanged. Although my canopy was now fully developed I faced another problem. My right leg hung straight down with the kitbag on it and I was quite unable to reach the grip to pull it up again.

Down below was a scene of orderly confusion as myriads of ant-like figures scurried over the DZ towards the different coloured flares marking battalion rendezvous areas. The sounds of shouts and shots drifted up, punctuated by bursts of machine-gun fire. The Americans had dropped us right on target and I had no difficulty in locating the yellow flare which showed where the 2nd Battalion was forming up. Everywhere order was developing out of seeming chaos as the airborne soldiers quickly organised themselves. The ground, which a moment before had seemed so far beneath me, came spinning up at an alarming rate. I was not looking forward to the landing, as my leg still dangled helplessly below me, weighted down with the kitbag. We had been told that to land in this way would almost certainly result in a broken leg, and any second I was going to find out.

Wham! I hit the deck with a terrific jolt, but all in one piece, and immediately struggled out of my parachute harness, slicing through the cords that held my kitbag to pull out my rifle. That was the first priority. In the distance time-bombs exploded, sending up great fountains of earth. They had been dropped twenty-four hours previously in an effort to persuade the Germans that this was just another bombing raid. Some hopes! Something glinted in the sun not thirty yards away: it was a rifle levelled straight at me. To my relief a very cockney voice shouted, 'What battalion, mate?' 'Second,' I croaked. 'Over to your right about two hundred yards. OK?' 'Thanks a lot,' I shouted, 'but who are you?' 'Independent Company. We're holding the DZ until you're all off it.'

We wished each other good luck and I hoisted the sixty pounds of mortar bombs on to my back, together with the pick, shovel, rifle and small pack. Looking like a Christmas tree, I set off in search of the 2nd Battalion. I met Sergeant Kalikoff, who appeared upset over something. When I asked what the trouble was he replied that he had lost his kitbag. At the thought of all those tedious and sweaty afternoons I burst out laughing. Maurice couldn't see the joke and told me to get moving.

About fifty yards ahead I spotted Slapsie blithely pushing along one of our collapsible tubular steel and canvas barrows. I called to him but my voice was drowned in the general din. Everyone appeared to be running in different directions but men became sections and then platoons. The latter became companies which were rapidly turning into battalions. My spine felt as though it would snap in two. Although Slapsie was no further from me he just would not look round. Every now and again a stray kitbag which had been insecurely fastened came whistling down to half-bury itself in the ground. One wondered what the odds were against being hit by a falling kitbag or a container plummeting to earth in this fashion, as there was so much stuff dropping out of the sky. In fact it was all so wonderful and exciting that one really had to make an effort to get on instead of standing there watching.

I had almost given up hope of reaching Slapsie when he unexpectedly stopped, turned round and wiped his brow. I jumped in the air and yelled his name as loud as I could and then went down on my knees under the weight of all I was carrying. At last Slapsie saw me and he waited patiently until I caught up with him. 'Wotcher, Kid, seen any of the others?' 'Only Maurice and he's rounding up stragglers.'

Slapsie told me to put my bombs on the barrow and give him a hand in pulling it. Presently we met Lieutenant Woods and other members of the platoon. More bombs were placed on the barrow and willing hands seized the toggle ropes while Slapsie held the handles. This was more like it. We crossed a path and passed a paratrooper from the 1st Battalion who was lying there with a broken leg. The medics were attending to him. A Dutch civilian came up, the first we had seen. He was impeccably dressed in a sort of tweed suit with a brown felt hat and spoke very good English. He warned us that there were six German armoured cars in the vicinity; as he spoke we could hear their powerful engines revving up.

We left the open path and doubled across a ploughed field to gain the comparative shelter of some trees. It was heavy going and we cursed the weight of the barrow which was slowing us down. Slapsie reminded us of the old joke, 'Work like a horse, might as well look like one.' This made us all laugh and in this cheerful state we eventually arrived at the 2nd Battalion rendezvous, to be greeted by the ironic cheers of those already there.

Chapter 3

ATTACK

COLONEL FROST came across to Lieutenant Woods to find out if we had suffered any casualties, but apart from several men who were missing we had had none so far. He then gave the order for the advance on Arnhem and the rifle companies began to move off. We were to bring up the rear with our 3-inch mortars as their supporting artillery. A number of Germans had already been captured. Dressed in their best Sunday uniforms, they were, at that moment, probably the most embarrassed soldiers in the German Army. They had been caught in the fields where we had landed, snogging with their Dutch girl friends, and their faces went redder and redder by the minute as they caught the drift of some of the remarks the grinning paratroopers flung at them.

'Right, on your feet!' came a shout, and we moved off in single file in sections on either side of the road in what was called 'ack-ack' formation. The Dutch countryside was very neat and well kept for wartime, the roads being overhung with trees and the fields fenced off with wire. Houses were scattered here and there and the inhabitants came out with their children to wave to us and watch us pass. Jugs of milk, apples, tomatoes and marigolds were pressed on us. They stuck the flowers in the scrim netting of our helmets and decorated our barrows with them. 'We have waited for you for four years,' seemed to be the limit of their English but the phrase was repeated over and over again by these smiling friendly people, who seemed to consider the war as good as finished now that we had arrived.

We pushed on south of the Wolfheze district where we had landed, in the direction of Heelsum. The bracken-covered heath on each side of the road rendered our exposed thrust very liable to ambush, and indeed not far ahead there was a burst of small-arms fire which sent us scurrying for cover. Leading elements of the battalion had made contact with the enemy, but the firing soon stopped and we pressed on. When we reached the scene of the skirmish the smoke and smell of cordite still lingered in the air. By the side of the road lay a tall fair-haired sergeant from one of the rifle companies; I recognised him as an ex-Guardsman who had been on the anti-tank gun course at Street when I was there. Now his face was blanched with pain and shock. He had caught a burst of machine-gun fire down one leg and his comrades had bandaged him up before leaving him. As we passed we murmured words of encouragement and threw him boiled sweets and cigarettes. The next time I saw him was in Stalag XIB, minus that leg.

Yet another burst of fire sent us diving for cover again but this time it was our lads who had done the firing. A German staff car was stopped on the road, the windscreen shattered and the tyres shot to pieces. A German officer lay dead in one of the front seats. Beside him, hunched over the steering wheel, was the driver. In the back was the body of another German officer slumped forward with his hand still on the shoulder of the dead driver. He had clearly been in the act of warning him when the British paratroopers had stepped out into the road in front of them and opened fire. The officer in the front seat appeared to be some sort of general, so this must have been a severe blow to the enemy.[1] I approached the staff car filled with curiosity, for not only had I never seen a German officer before but I had never seen a corpse. My parents had protected me from such sights by the face-saving phrase, 'No thanks, I'd rather remember him as I saw him last.'

My mother had told me as a child that if I traced the shape of

---

[1] James Sims is convinced, having studied official photographs of the incident published after the war, that this officer was General Kussin, *Stadtkommandant* of Arnhem. Kussin's car, however, was ambushed by men of the 3rd Battalion and there is some doubt as to whether the author could actually have passed it. General Frost confirms that there was a 'scuppered staff car' on the 2nd Battalion's route but it has not been possible to establish whether it was, in fact, the Citroen belonging to Kussin.

a cross on the forehead of a corpse I would not dream about it. Gingerly I touched the stone-cold forehead of one of the German officers. 'What the hell are you doing?' yelled a sergeant. 'Get mobile, you'll see plenty more like him before you're much older!'

We reached a village, which might have been Heelsum. Here we ran into our worst ambush yet and the Mortar Platoon received its personal baptism of fire. On the left-hand side of the road was a hedge about seven feet high and on the other a row of red-brick houses on a higher road. There was the usual enthusiastic demonstration by the local inhabitants and more flowers. Lieutenant Woods, who was leading the platoon, had just reached a house at the further end of the hedge when a woman suddenly screamed from one of the overlooking houses and ran inside, slamming the door.

As though this was a signal the hedge was raked from end to end belly-high by machine-gun fire. Although the enemy could not see us they hit at least three of our lads, one of them with an incendiary bullet. This was the youthful Brum Davis. The rest of us had already flattened ourselves on the tarmac but my helmet seemed to stick up an awful long way as the bullets swept over us again and again. It was a terrifying experience, as we were lying on top of the road and there was no ditch to crawl into. Our only hope was that with Jerry firing blind we might escape. All we could hear was the fiendish whine of the bullets and the sobbing moans of our wounded comrades.

Lieutenant Woods, having reached the dubious shelter of the house at the other end of the hedge, stood up and emptied a whole clip of .45 ammunition in the direction of the enemy, at the same time ordering us to make a dash for it. We scrambled to our feet and I seized hold of the handles of one of our barrows while others dragged it to the comparative protection of the house. The firing ceased as the German machine-gun crew departed, having achieved what they set out to do – hold us up. Despite the hail of bullets the Dutch civilians had turned out to aid the wounded, whom we left in their care; but Brum was dead. At nineteen his great adventure was over before it had scarcely begun.

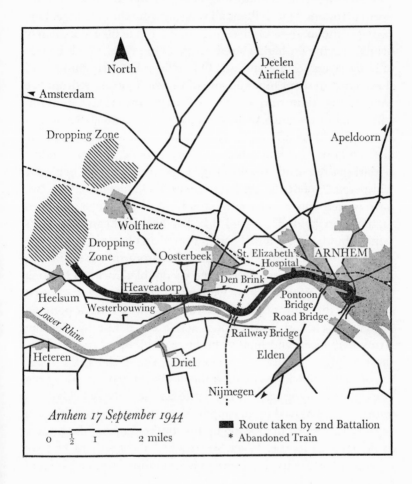

North

◄ Amsterdam

Deelen
Airfield

Dropping Zone

Apeldoorn

Wolfheze

Dropping
Zone

Oosterbeek

St. Elizabeth's
Hospital

ARNHEM

Heaveadorp

Den Brink

Heelsum

Westerbouwing

Pontoon
Bridge
Road Bridge

*

Lower Rhine

Railway Bridge

Heteren

Driel

Elden

Nijmegen ►

Arnhem 17 September 1944

0   ½   1   2 miles

■■ Route taken by 2nd Battalion
* Abandoned Train

The lieutenant ordered us to press on, but this became more and more difficult the further we got into Arnhem. Crowds were now greeting us as liberators as if the war was already over. We were surrounded by civilians all wearing something orange. One young Dutchman was charging about on a bike completely drunk, waving on high a stone bottle of gin from which he was offering swigs to one and all. Our officer lost his temper and threatened to shoot him and any of us who touched a drop. We were losing time and he seemed to realise that this semi-triumphal entry into Arnhem would not last much longer. If there were to be any more ambushes he wanted us to be fully alert and our reactions unimpaired by alcohol. From a window a dark-haired and beautiful girl gazed down at me and whispered 'Goodbye.' At least it was a change from the 'we have waited four years' routine but it made me shiver. I turned to the man behind me and asked if he had heard the girl's remark but he just grinned and muttered an obscenity.

At last we were able to free ourselves from the embarrassing attentions of our Dutch friends and we doubled forward to catch up with the riflemen who were now approaching their first objective, the railway bridge. Beyond this there was a pontoon bridge, which had been thrown across the Rhine by German Army engineers, and finally the huge single-span road bridge, the real prize. Shouts, screams, cheers, single shots, the rapid fire of enemy machine guns and the slower reply of our own Bren guns came echoing back as the battle for the railway bridge was joined. As we moved up in support there was a terrific explosion as Jerry succeeded in blowing up the southern end of the bridge, so denying us its use. When we reached the northern end we found, still on the tracks, a very fine streamlined train which had been abandoned.

The now familiar smell of spent ammunition lingered in the air and a pall of smoke hung over the scene of what had clearly been a short sharp engagement. The riflemen had hurried on to the next objective, the pontoon bridge, but they had left one of their number behind. He lay propped up against a wooden seat in a clearing overlooking the river. It was a pleasant spot, shaded by trees, with a beautiful view over the Lower Rhine, the sort of place where lovers plan their future and old men dream of the past. But today there were here neither lovers nor old men, only a boy from a rifle company, his legs buckled under him and his helmet removed. The front of his battle blouse was soaked with blood, and someone with rough well-meaning had stuffed a white towel inside the front of his shirt in a vain attempt to staunch the wound. Out of a waxen face his eyes stared steadily past us into eternity and we crept by as quietly as possible as though afraid of waking him from that dread sleep. Some of our lads who were Catholics crossed themselves.

We were coming into the outskirts of Arnhem when yet another hidden machine gunner sent us sprawling on top of one another in the nearest ditch. Laughing and cursing we sorted ourselves out, peering over our rifle sights into the matted hedgerows beyond. Nothing moved. The click of a rifle bolt being cocked sounded almost sacrilegious in the cathedral-like silence which followed the enemy burst of fire. Before my eyes two ants were busy on a recce, trying first this path and then another through the interlocking grasses. Their minute antennae twitched ceaselessly like tiny radio aerials as they darted about. They could easily have been destroyed between finger and thumb but I had a strange fellow feeling for those ants. Perhaps they too were shock troops for some hidden ant army awaiting the signal to advance. Maybe some omnipotent deity was watching me in the same way and wondering whether or not to pinch out my life or allow me to fulfil my shallow destiny.

These reflections were rudely shattered by a cry from the head of the column – 'Tanks!' No warning strikes more fear into the lightly armed infantryman; St George was better armed to meet his dragon than we were to take on the mighty enemy panzers. The cry was passed down the column until it reached the Anti-Tank Section, who piled into a jeep and came careering down the road whooping and cheering as they made ready with their Piats, as though attempting to knock out enemy AFVs was great fun. They vanished round a bend in the road and there followed a succession of shots and shouts, punctuated by a single loud explosion. The menace had been dealt with.

As we rose to our feet again General Urquhart, the commander of the 1st Airborne Division, came tearing up in a jeep, which he was driving himself, and skidded to a halt alongside us. The general looked tough and genial, seemingly confident and in a good humour as he asked the whereabouts of Colonel Frost. We told him the colonel was up at the front of the attack and with a wave and a shout of 'Good luck!' he drove off at high speed with his ashen-faced aide beside him.

We now took another road which led down by the river. The Germans spotted us from the opposite side and opened fire with heavy machine guns. They were firing at very long range, and when we dropped down off the road into an adjacent field they seemed to lose us. They fired hundreds of rounds, most of which passed harmlessly over our heads. We were completely without cover, but in our camouflaged smocks we were invisible against the background and suffered no casualties. What was most important, we kept moving in spite of this very heavy fire, the only effect of which was to stampede some cattle.

We moved forward swiftly in the wake of the riflemen. Ahead we could hear the sounds of battle as they fought for possession of the pontoon bridge. Another terrific explosion told us that once more Jerry had beaten us to it. When we reached the northern end of the bridge we saw that quite a scrap had taken place, and a number of dead and wounded Germans lay about. There was no sign of the riflemen, who had already pushed on towards the last unblown bridge over the Rhine, in the centre of Arnhem. Some of the German casualties were SS men, distinguishable by the runes on their collars. I was curious to see what these supermen looked like but, apart from their uniform, they were just like us. One of them was badly wounded but still alive; he was terrified we were going to shoot him. He was screaming and carrying on something shocking. Lieutenant Woods told him to shut up and ordered one of our medics to have a look at him. Nevertheless he continued to raise the roof, so the lieutenant waved his .45 in the SS man's face. This had the desired effect.

We halted at the pontoon bridge for some time and took the opportunity to have something to eat. By now it was growing

dark and we had been in action for several hours, although with
so much happening it didn't seem so long. I felt exhausted, and
put it down to all the extra excitement and the fact that we had
parachuted into battle. When joining the Parachute Regiment
we had been told that one parachute jump was equal to eight
hours' manual labour; by this time I was ready to believe it.
Lieutenant Woods appeared with a German Army bicycle that
he had found and a stick grenade which he gave into my care.
I accepted them grudgingly, especially the bike, as it was hardly
safe to ride it and made taking cover that much more difficult.

Our Machine Gun Platoon had set up two of their Vickers
guns to cover the enemy-held side of the river. Soon we heard
the chug of a motor boat coming up river. To our amazement a
small German patrol boat hove into view. The crew seemed
quite unaware that anything unusual was happening in Arnhem
that Sunday. One soldier was leaning over the stern smoking a
pipe, at peace with the world.

Commands rang out and we heard the snap of the Vickers'
cocking levers. Another order brought the guns to life. At such
short range they pulverised the enemy boat. The pipe-smoker
at the stern just toppled over the guard rail into the Rhine. I
don't suppose he knew what hit him. The boat heeled over and
sank in seconds. From the fuss our rival platoon made you
would have thought they had sunk the *Scharnhorst*.

While all this was going on our riflemen had been re-forming
for the attack on the final and most essential objective of all, the
road bridge. We could see the top of its huge single span, which
dominated the surrounding buildings at a point where the river
curved sharply.

We knew that the Germans must be working feverishly to set
charges to blow it up before the cobra-like head of the 2nd
Battalion, snaking along the river road, reached it. So far our
advance into Arnhem had resembled the action of a serpent,
coiling up and then striking, a bridge at a time. The Germans
had succeeded in blowing up two of the three bridges, so it was
imperative to capture this one. HQ Company, which included
our platoon, was ordered to close up behind what remained of
the riflemen for the final assault, as by this time 'A' and 'B'

Companies had been mauled and 'C' Company had completely disappeared.

We set off on the last lap, moving from one piece of cover to another. A German machine gun sent us diving behind a low brick wall. We looked up to see Joe Hamilton, our newest sergeant, standing over us: 'What the hell are you doing down there? Come on, get out of it!' We shuffled to our feet, the enemy gunners having faded away after delaying us for a few more seconds. It was growing darker now and we were correspondingly jumpier. Much to my relief, the lieutenant told me to get rid of the bike. Those not on the barrows covered the men trudging along the road. An airborne engineer attached himself to Slapsie and me and offered to help with the barrow if we would let him put his Bren gun on it. I welcomed his offer as I had pushed that darned barrow since our first ambush and was glad of a break.

We pressed on, flitting from door to door. All of a sudden I received a fleeting impression of grey behind me. I stiffened, expecting either a bayonet or a burst of Schmeisser fire. Nothing happened and I spun round and lunged with the bayonet, narrowly missing a slim young Dutch girl wearing a grey jumper and black slacks. She could not have been more than sixteen and looked a real tomboy, though a scared one. My relief turned to anger at the fright she had given me and I bundled her back inside her front door with a few well-chosen words. Slapsie roared with laughter and said it was no way to treat a lady.

We left the quayside and branched up into the town again between two tall blocks of flats. People looked down on us from their windows and waved, but without the enthusiasm of the country folk. Perhaps they could foresee that their beautiful town would be laid in ruins before long. Even so some of these Dutch civilians took quite extraordinary risks to warn us of enemy activity or snipers.

The lieutenant's batman had been one of those wounded in an earlier ambush and he asked me to accompany him in his place; I was a newcomer to the battalion and just a bomb-carrier, so I would not be missed. I now found myself at the head of the platoon right behind the officer, a most uncomfortable position. We were crossing a road when there was a sudden burst of fire. A stream of tracer bullets passed so close to us that they lit up the lieutenant's face. I grabbed at his shoulder to pull him back but he had already reacted and dashed for cover with the rest of us as the enemy fire narrowly missed our backsides.

Now we were cut off from the rifle companies but at that moment George Hines brought up the Bren gun carrier, our platoon transport. Lieutenant Woods jumped aboard, ordering George to take her round the corner and head straight for the enemy machine-gun nest. As the carrier tore off some wit remarked, 'Hope her tracks stay on. . . .' We all laughed, as back home the carriers had a nasty habit of shedding a track when turned too sharply. However, on this occasion George cornered her faster than any of us had seen him do before – and the tracks stayed on. Lieutenant Woods fired straight down the throats of the enemy while we dodged past the back of the carrier to gain the shelter of the houses beyond.

From the direction of the road bridge came the confused roar of the fiercest fighting yet. We heard not only the now familiar sounds of shots, explosions and screams but something else as well, the battle cry of the 1st Para Brigade – 'Waho Mohammed!' 'Waho Mohammed!' – a cry that had been adopted during the North African fighting and was already familiar to the Germans.

All caution was now forgotten as battle fever gripped us and we swept forward led by our platoon sergeant Sergeant Jackman. The lieutenant was coming up with the carrier and we knew we had to get that bridge whatever happened. The firing appeared to be slackening off up front but who had given best, us or Jerry? The riflemen had already suffered many casualties on the way in. We ran on past an SS police barracks, which was now on fire. Several of Hitler's black-uniformed thugs lay dead on the path outside. In the gutter lay two more dead in the less familiar Luftwaffe blue. They were a boy and a girl of about my own age. The boy was slumped across a light machine gun with the girl beside him, the ammunition belt threaded through her fingers. The girl's blonde hair was stained with blood; they had died quickly and violently. Who were they? Brother and sister? Lovers? It was just another of those war-time incidents that made a mockery of fiction.

There was now less than a hundred yards to go to the bridge, but our pace slackened when we saw that our comrades had already taken the northern end of it. The Germans had been surprised while laying charges and driven off, but the riflemen had suffered heavily in the process, as the enemy had cannon mounted in pill-boxes. The airborne engineers put paid to these with their flame-throwers.

The depleted and almost exhausted riflemen had also cleared out some of the houses surrounding the northern end of the bridge. The Germans had broken and run, leaving guns, trucks and ammunition in our hands. The scratch force they had col-lected together to defend the bridge had been no match for the riflemen. There was only some desultory firing as we started to occupy the houses which had already been cleared. The Mortar Platoon was allocated a large house on the left-hand side of the road and the Machine Gun Platoon a warehouse just west of the bridge with a commanding view of the southern approaches to it.

HQ was set up in another large building, believed to have been a school, about two houses along on the same side of the road as the Mortar Platoon house and with a very good view of the northern end of the bridge. We had also captured the local morgue. The dying were quickly removed from the streets and cleared away out of sight, for the time being at any rate.

By now it was quite dark but the whole area was illuminated by the fires from burning German vehicles which had tried to make a dash across the bridge and had been stopped by our lads. Over everything loomed the bridge, for which so many men had already died and for whose possession many more were to die in the following days. We were under orders to hold on until the arrival of Second Army, which was scheduled for midday on 18 September. We felt quite pleased with ourselves for we had dropped over sixty miles behind the enemy lines, fought our way into a large town and captured the northern end of our main objective, the road bridge.

We no longer had the strength or the weapons to capture the southern end but we felt certain that we could prevent Jerry blowing the bridge or crossing it. Now it was up to our main army, which had already crossed the Dutch frontier, to make the final thrust and to relieve us without further delay. Our Mortar Platoon casualties had been light considering the distance from the dropping zone to the bridge, and we had reached it with two out of our four mortars and plenty of ammunition.

There was an island of grass with shrubs and trees in the centre of the road west of the bridge. Lieutenant Woods selected this for our mortar position. He ordered us to dig two pits for the mortars and to surround these with slit-trenches. Sergeant Kalikoff was left to organise this while the lieutenant went off to inspect the house which was to be held by the rest of the platoon, and to see if its defence had been properly organised. Opposite our house, on the far side of our island, was a large light-grey warehouse which was now manned by survivors of the rifle companies and the airborne engineers. For the remainder of the action the sappers were to fight as infantry alongside the riflemen.

Slapsie and I started to dig a slit-trench with our entrenching tools on the side of the island overlooked by the Mortar Platoon house. The soil was very sandy and easy to shift, but I felt so exhausted that I kept grumbling about the job and asking Slapsie every other minute how much deeper we had to go. He took little notice of my belly-aching and kept at it like a mole, only pausing to say, 'Two or three hours from now and it won't seem half deep enough!' These were to be prophetic words.

Just as I thought I couldn't dig another spadeful Slapsie straightened up and OK'd the trench. Round its lip we had raised a mound, leaving slots for our rifles. Gradually all the parachutists disappeared as, like sexton beetles, they burrowed deeper and deeper into the earth. A quiet settled over the island. Slapsie and I eased ourselves down and sat facing each other with our feet touching. I took out of my pack a large piece of Army fruit cake which I had thoughtfully included when packing, and we shared it. Having dried out a bit it tasted quite good. Usually when served back home it was rather soggy and got left on the mess-room tables, only to be collected up by the cooks and presented the following day covered with custard, disguised as a sweet.

On the bridge vehicles were still burning. One was obviously an ammunition lorry. Every now and again it shuddered as the fire reached a further box of bullets or shells and they exploded. The small arms ammo spiralled away into the night sky like a gigantic catherine wheel; it was a fantastic firework display. Each successive explosion illuminated the immediate area and I saw some stocky confident-looking riflemen already setting off on an offensive patrol. A pall of thick black smoke from the burning trucks hung over our positions. Although it smelt bad, it did help to conceal us from the enemy. On the road near our island a sentry from one of the rifle companies paced up and down, his heel-plates clinking softly on the street – one indication of the measure of control we had established around the northern end of the bridge.

After supper we decided to take turns in keeping watch. I was so tired that Slapsie suggested he took the first turn, which suited me fine. He promised to wake me so that I could do my stint of duty, but, being a good-natured bloke and feeling sorry for me, he actually let me sleep all through the night.

My chin slowly sank on to my chest and I started to doze off. From what seemed a long way off came the crackle of exploding ammo. It was like drifting into sleep after a particularly good Bonfire Night when there are still one or two enthusiasts throwing the last squibs on a dying fire.

Chapter 4

COUNTER-ATTACK

I AWOKE early on the morning of 18 September to find Slapsie regarding me with a look of awe and respect. The reason for this was that we had been attacked during the night by Jerry; at the height of the battle Slapsie had tried desperately to wake me, but all in vain. I had slept on while the remainder of the men on the island repelled the attack. At one point poor Slapsie had been forced to kneel on me to fire, but he said that I might just as well have been dead for all the response I gave. One might have supposed that he would be very annoyed but in fact he now regarded me as a very cool customer indeed. I only hoped that I could live up to this new image.

We were both chilled by a cold mist which had come up off the Rhine, obscuring everything. There wasn't a sound and it seemed as if we were the only two men still there. Although we could barely see the Mortar Platoon house, we knew that our lads would be watching for the enemy and covering us as well. As the mist swirled about I could make out several crumpled grey-clad heaps lying in the road just beyond the perimeter of the island, a pathetic reminder of the German night attack.

Slapsie gripped my arm and hissed, 'Someone behind us!' My back hair stood on end as we twisted in our narrow slit-trench to meet this new emergency. We both breathed a sigh of relief as Lieutenant Woods loomed out of the mist. He knelt down and smiled at us. 'Had a good night?' We nodded. 'Good. I want you to come with me, Sims. We're going down to the Machine Gun Platoon to set up an OP. I want you to lay this telephone line from here to their place.'

So saying, he gave me a drum of telephone wire which I put on my bayonet to ensure an easier payout. I was loath to leave

the shelter of the slit-trench and the reassuring company of
Slapsie, but as the lieutenant's unofficial batman I had little
choice in the matter. Being a batman was quite a cushy number
back in camp but it was not so cushy stumbling about in the
mist-shrouded streets of enemy-held territory at seven in the
morning.

Leaving one end of the wire with Slapsie, together with a
portable telephone, we set off. The lieutenant led the way. The
mist enveloped us like a cloak – the island had already vanished
– but he seemed to know where he was going so all I had to
do was stick close to him and keep paying out the line. He
had a radio with a long whip-aerial strapped around him,
a telephone under his left arm and a .45 automatic in his right
hand. The closer we came to the Machine Gun Platoon the
thicker grew the mist, for we were quite near the Rhine. Lieutenant Woods kept going at the same steady but cautious rate.
We seemed to be making a hell of a noise with our boots and at
every step I expected to be cut down by a panzer grenadier.
We were eventually challenged by an alert sapper sentry, who
gave us as much gen as he could on the position ahead. We came
to a small back gate on the left-hand side of the road, which led
into a yard adjoining the warehouse held by the machine
gunners.

Unfortunately there was no connecting door and we had to
negotiate a six-foot wall. We found some barrels and rolled one
against it. Lieutenant Woods went up first. He was soon astride
the top of the wall, but his radio aerial became caught up in
what looked like a clothes line. He cursed the offending item;
to me, crouched down below awaiting my turn to ascend, his
voice sounded as blasphemous as someone shouting out in the
middle of solemn High Mass in Westminster Cathedral. At last
he succeeded in freeing the aerial and stretched his hand down
to help me up. We wasted no time in scrambling over that
particular wall. We heard the sound of a bolt being cocked by
yet another alert sentry, who challenged us before letting us
past the heavily-barricaded rear entrance of the warehoue. It
took the machine gunners fully five minutes to make a gap large
enough for us to scrape through.

We were directed to the upper storeys where the main body of the Machine Gun Platoon was posted. We climbed the stairs and found the guns set up, with a good field of fire, in two rooms overlooking the southern approaches to the road bridge. The ugly snouts of the Vickers heavy machine guns poked through the open windows, while their crews fussed over them to make sure everything would be OK for what they were hoping would be some lively action. Although we of the Support Company were not noted for our dash and *élan* in the way that the Rifle Companies were, we were just as keen and efficient, and I knew that back on the island the same careful preparations were being made in readiness for the expected German counter-attack as soon as the mist lifted.

Lieutenant Woods and the Machine Gun Platoon officer were good friends off duty. They were glad to see each other, and we were offered every facility to set up our observation post. Unfortunately when we came to test our portable telephone we discovered that it was out of order and nothing we could do would make it work. The machine gunners did not have a spare one. Lieutenant Woods was so furious over this that he flung the useless instrument at the nearest wall, making a devil of a clatter. Everyone looked instinctively at the bridge, which we could dimly discern through the rapidly lifting mist. There was no sign of life from Jerry and I doubt if at that moment there were any Germans on the bridge. 'We'll have to find somewhere nearer the gun pits and use the walkie-talkie,' said the lieutenant.

As we took our leave of the machine gunners I fancied that some of them were not sorry to see the backs of such noisy guests. 'What about the wire, sir?' I asked. 'Leave it where it is,' replied my officer. 'Perhaps some German will trip over it and break his bloody neck.'

We made our way back to the island quickly, for the morning sun was dispersing the mist and stray shots warned us that the warming-up for a renewal of the fighting had begun. We reached the 'White House', which was the name given to the large light-grey warehouse immediately opposite our positions, held by 2nd Battalion riflemen and airborne engineers. Lieutenant Woods had a word with Sergeant Hamilton, who was now on the island with the mortar crews, saying that he would set up an OP in the White House and relay fire orders by walkie-talkie. The reason that we had not stayed down by the river was that we had found difficulty in contacting the island by radio; when the heavy machine guns started up communication would have been almost impossible. We didn't seem to be having much luck with our radio sets and yet previously in England they had worked all right. It was a mystery why we were having such trouble over these short distances: perhaps the large buildings which surrounded us were the cause.

To get into the White House we had to climb through a window in the side-street we had just walked down, as the front of the house was already under heavy fire. We had barely reached safety when we heard a flurry of shots outside, coupled with the roar of powerful armoured car engines being revved up. These sounds came from the west, the direction from which we had entered Arnhem, thus indicating that we were now cut off from the remainder of the 1st Airborne Division. However, as airborne troops, we expected this at certain stages of a battle and it was of no particular significance at that moment. We climbed some stairs and stepped into a large room overlooking our island. Two bullets ricocheted off the window barricades, narrowly missing us as we dived for the floor together in a cloud of dust. From the depths of an armchair a wounded officer surveyed us critically. 'Snipers,' he told us. 'While you're over here you'll find it safer to crawl on your belly.'

He wore no beret or steel helmet and was badly hit in one shoulder. His wounded arm was strapped up in a highly-coloured sling improvised from a Paisley shawl, which made a vivid splash of colour against his camouflage jacket. His voice was steady, his jaw set, but his eyes told of the pain which swept over him at intervals, during which he wandered in his speech. Lieutenant Woods told him why we were there and offered him some brandy, which he refused. He lost his temper with one of his own men whom he wanted to have a look at some houses believed to be held by the enemy. He ordered the man to use field glasses for this purpose but after seeing the bullets ricochet off the barricades the man was understandably reluctant to comply, as the glint of the sun on the glasses would be a dead give-away to the sniper. It was clear that he regarded his officer as a bit round the bend to expect him to take this risk, and made no allowance for his condition. 'Observe, damn you!' shouted the officer, waving his .45 at the man in a very threatening manner. Lieutenant Woods intervened and told me to take the glasses off the rifleman and observe. I did so, focusing on the barricade about three inches in front of me while I pretended to report German activity in the suspect house across the road. Although I saw no sign of life I was pretty sure that the Germans were in the house in question. This seemed to satisfy the wounded officer, who sank back into his chair again.

There was nothing further we could do, so we left him and made our way up to the attic. This was a splendid room as it was unoccupied and commanded extensive views of the southern approach to the bridge from the back and of our island position from the front. The front window was very small but from it I could see our lads getting the mortar bombs ready for firing. We dragged a sideboard to a position underneath the rear window. Lieutenant Woods set up his map and began to work out the distances from our gun positions to various targets on the other side of the river. At this point Jerry started to shell us, driving us downstairs for a while.

We returned to the room dominated by the Byronic-looking figure in the armchair. Now the Germans launched a determined infantry attack down the road facing us, which was a branch of the one leading directly to the bridge from the north. They made straight for us but evidently did not realise that some of the houses on their right flank were occupied by paratroopers. They were lorried infantry and it was a bold attack, but many of the Germans died in their trucks and those that tried to escape were shot down before they they could reach cover.

One terribly wounded German soldier, shot through both legs, pulled himself hand over hand towards his own lines. We watched his slow and painful progress with horrified fascination, as he was the only creature moving among a carpet of the dead.

He pulled himself across the road, and over the pavement, then dragged his shattered body inch by inch up a grass-covered incline leading to the bridge road. Once he had cleared a slight parapet at the top of the incline he would be back in his own lines. He must have been in terrible pain but he conquered the incline by sheer will-power. With a superhuman effort he heaved himself up to clear the final obstacle. A rifle barked out next to me and I watched in disbelief as the wounded German fell back, shot through the head. To me it was little short of murder but to my companion, a Welshman, one of our best snipers, the German was a legitimate target. When I protested he looked at me as though I was simple.

Shortly after the failure of the first German infantry attack a white civilian ambulance came hurtling down the same road towards us. An over-excited Bren gunner opened up and shot the front of it to pieces. 'Cease fire, you bloody fool!' yelled an officer. 'Can't you see the Red Cross?' Even as he spoke the back doors of the ambulance sprang open and a dozen fully armed SS men came tumbling out firing automatic weapons from the hip. They charged straight at us. 'Let 'em have it, lads!' yelled the officer. But the Brens and rifles were already at their grim task and not a man survived that desperate attempt. One fanatical SS trooper actually reached the front door of the White House before collapsing on the steps, riddled with bullets. By now the road was covered with dead and dying Germans. Our medics went out to clear the dead away and care for the wounded.

'Suppose they'll send a hearse next,' remarked one para-trooper, but after these failures by their infantry the Germans put down a sustained artillery and mortar bombardment. I gazed down on the island where our men were crouching in vulnerable-looking gun pits and slit-trenches. All around them shrapnel was pattering down like a thunderstorm of death, and yet, in spite of the small area of the island and the number of trenches on it, not one bomb or splinter hit anyone. It was a miracle. Although the German mortar bombs were not as powerful as ours a direct hit or near miss still meant death or being maimed for life.

The barrage lifted as suddenly as it had begun, and a column of light tanks and armoured cars manned by SS approached from the east along the road which led underneath the bridge and ran between our island and the White House. They attacked with great spirit, but we were lucky enough to have two 6-pounder anti-tank guns manned by the airborne artillery. Although they were on the open streets and were completely without any sort of cover apart from the gunshield, these gunners manhandled their guns to meet the new threat and with their first shot brought the leading enemy tank to a flaming halt. It slewed half round and came to a stop directly under the bridge, thus completely blocking the way for the following armour. As the tanks slowed down the paratroops poured a withering fire into them. The German AFVs were knocked out one after another as they tried desperately to disengage or negotiate the flaming metal coffins. Black smoke belched from the leading tank, now well ablaze, but any movement from our positions still brought a stream of well-aimed machine-gun fire from the turret guns. The paratroops shouted to the SS man to come out, promising to spare his life, for they were impressed by his fanatical courage. The only reply was a further burst of fire. As the flames got to him we could hear his screams of agony, muffled by the steel turret, but none the less disturbing for that. They seemed to go on for an awfully long time before this brave soldier died for Führer and Fatherland.

Following the spectacular failure of this attack the enemy tried to cross the bridge from the south with tanks, armoured cars and lorried infantry, but the paras repeated their tactics of knocking out the leading vehicle, completely stalling everything behind it. However, once under the girders of the bridge, the enemy were afforded quite an amount of cover and it proved difficult to hit them.

The time was barely ten o'clock and yet ages seemed to have passed since the lieutenant and I had strolled down the street outside. This was now a very hazardous place and we felt more than pleased with ourselves. Despite Jerry's local superiority in tanks and manpower, we had been giving him a good hiding. Of course the German tanks were at a disadvantage in street fighting as they had to be sent down concrete defiles manned by troops renowned for their skill in defensive action. We were ensconced in strongly built warehouses with plenty of ammunition, food and water. We had only to hang on until the main relieving army arrived according to schedule.

There is no doubt that the average British line regiment is at its best in defence, and we were not an average unit made up of a few regulars and a mass of conscripts, but all special volunteers. By 1944 the Parachute Regiment was one of the most experienced battle units in the whole Allied command. Although a newcomer to the battalion, with a total Army service of eighteen months, I had served with the 15th Sussex Battalion of the Home Guard before joining up. I had been trained in street fighting, which was now proving most useful.

One thing that surprised us was the speed of the German reaction to our landings and the appearance of the SS armour, for in our pre-operational briefing there was no mention of any tanks being in the Arnhem area. All that talk about Luftwaffe personnel and sub-standard line-of-communication troops! I doubt if there was any such animal as a sub-standard German soldier. Certainly those now outside our building and trying to break in didn't come into that category.

When the Germans found they couldn't get across the bridge they began to shell and mortar us once again, but we had few casualties as the houses we were in had been well constructed and seemed capable of absorbing terrific punishment. The mortaring was, however, a considerable strain on the nerves and as soon as it ceased the Germans switched on a factory siren, which continued to wail until the mortars opened up again. I didn't know which was worse. During a lull in the bombardment Lieutenant Woods decided to return to the attic to see if we could hit back with our 3-inch mortars. So far we had been unable to use them because Jerry was so close to us all the time. There were still a number of German vehicles on the bridge itself but owing to the girders they could not be got at.

The lieutenant noticed more lorried infantry approaching from the south and immediately decided to engage this dream target. Rapidly working out the range and elevation, he gave the necessary fire orders for me to transmit to Sergeant Hamilton down on the island. For some technical reason it was not possible to use the walkie-talkie for this purpose and in the end I had to lean out of the small front window and shout the orders down to Joe. This was a risky business with snipers about and Joe wondered where the devil the shouting was coming from until he spotted me and waved his acknowledgement. I waited just long enough to hear him bark out the orders and to see our lads put the bombs down the barrels of our drainpipes of death before joining my officer to observe the fall of shot. He passed me his field glasses so that I could have a look. I saw that we had set alight at least two trucks and that the others were trying to turn and get out of range as fast as possible. The enemy were jumping from the trucks and running for cover as our bombs landed on the target; it must have come as a terrific shock to be hit by such devastating fire from the other side of the river. The lieutenant lengthened the range to catch the retreating enemy and, once again, after passing the orders down to Joe I saw more trucks put out of action. The Machine Gun Platoon had also joined in and between us we soon destroyed this attempted build-up, the survivors fleeing at top speed.

The Germans recommenced mortaring and shelling. We in the White House were lucky to escape so lightly, for pieces of the external brickwork fell off and at each explosion or direct hit we were showered with plaster dust from walls and ceiling. Yet again the barrage lifted and the siren wailed, causing one soldier down below to suggest jokingly, 'How about a patrol to blow up the Arnhem laundry?' Another asked if we were on overtime as he had distinctly heard the 'knocking off' whistle.

A rather heavier bombardment drove us below again to the room on the ground floor through the side window of which we had entered the house. The riflemen had been told that Headquarters had been in touch with Second Army, and that XXX Corps, known as the Breakaway Corps, was trying to get through to us by midday on Tuesday. Another twenty-four hours . . . could we hold out that long? What had gone wrong? Evidently things were not going quite as planned with the relieving army.

Neither Lieutenant Woods nor I had eaten so far that day and he told me to make a stew from the dehydrated meat cubes and biscuits that we carried. Moreover, I was not to use the water in our water bottles but to find out if any was available in the White House. I soon discovered to my dismay that the only supply of water was from a tap on the end of a four-foot high pipe in the middle of the backyard, over which a furious exchange of fire was taking place. I was assured, however, by the defenders of this area that provided I dashed some of the way and then pushed myself along on my side for the remainder of the journey I would be quite safe unless someone lobbed a grenade.

The barriers were removed and I did as instructed. I found myself lying under the tap with my two mess tins, while a few feet overhead the air was full of bullets. I managed to turn the tap on; of course the water fell as much on me as in the mess tins. No doubt the Germans knew that directly underneath the tap, although out of sight, was an idiot who sooner or later would have to reach up and turn it off, and then . . . However, I not only filled both mess tins but managed to turn off the tap and returned to the rear entrance of the White House unscathed, pushing the mess tins in front of me. The riflemen and engineers cheered as I got safely back inside.

I returned to our room and set up the tommy cooker, an ingenious piece of equipment which used solid fuel tablets and would boil water in no time at all. I powdered the dehydrated meat and mixed it with shrapnel-like fragments of Army biscuits in one of the mess tins of water. I then brought the whole ghastly concoction to the boil, watched by a most unenthusiastic Lieutenant Woods. When it was ready I handed the tin to the lieutenant to have first taste. He gingerly took a spoonful, tasted it, and with a grimace of disgust spat it out. He then reached into his pack, took out a half-pound slab of chocolate and broke it solemnly in half, one piece of which he gave to me without a word. We ate in silence and I was grateful that he made no comment on my cooking. Perhaps he was afraid that I might do for him before he could get to grips with the enemy.

The lieutenant decided to return to the attic to see if we could spot the positions of any enemy guns or mortars. The German fire had begun to increase both in weight and in accuracy even while we had been eating, and although our gun pits were still intact some shells and mortar bombs had at last succeeded in penetrating the walls and roofs of our houses, causing casualties. Luckily, as far as we knew, none of these was fatal, the bursting power of the German ammunition being relatively poor compared with our own. Several in fact failed to go off, thus lending strength to the propaganda tales we were always being told of Czech and other foreign slave labourers in Nazi factories filling shells and bombs with sand instead of explosive.

We took it in turns to scan the far banks of the Rhine for signs of the enemy, but nothing suspicious caught my eye. It was Lieutenant Woods who first spotted something. 'Here, take a look at that low red-brick building directly opposite,' he said, at the same handing me his field glasses. From behind the building came three distinct puffs of smoke. Jerry had a mortar concealed there, thus utilising one of this weapon's greatest advantages – its howitzer-like ability to lob a bomb over anything. Jerry was particularly proficient with the mortar and the paras who had already experienced his handling of it in North Africa and Sicily used to say, 'Hold your mess tin out half a mile away and Jerry will put the third bomb in it.' Our men were just as keen as the enemy and after receiving the necessary fire orders quickly got their bombs off. Lieutenant Woods and I had the satisfaction of seeing the enemy mortar and its crew tossed into the air as our bombs scored a direct hit. We thought a bomb must have landed smack on their base plate to achieve such drastic results.

Shortly after this the Germans increased their artillery barrage once more and started to fire on us from the other side of the Rhine. When pieces of shrapnel came through the roof and blew out the rear windows the lieutenant decided to quit the attic. Downstairs we were rather surprised to meet another member of our platoon, a Scots sergeant, who had been trying unsuccessfully to rig up a wireless set. He told us that in spite of the shelling, casualties both on the island and in the Mortar Platoon house were light and that everyone was still very cheerful and optimistic about the way things were going.

About 4 pm we received a visit from Colonel Frost who had

crossed the road with a party of his officers, exchanging fire with the enemy *en route*. He radiated confidence but I overheard him dispatch someone down to the river bank to ascertain the state of some barges he knew were there. Meanwhile he came round and spoke to us and evidently satisfied himself about the defensive measures we had taken. He seemed to be highly pleased with the general situation. Presently the man who had been down to the Rhine to look at the barges returned with the news that they were a complete write-off, having been damaged by the Germans.

'That's that, then,' said the colonel, 'we'll stay where we are.' I wondered if he had been thinking how we might escape from the bridge if the Second Army didn't put in an appearance, but there was nothing in his manner to suggest this. He might just as well have been considering the use of these barges to cross the Rhine and take the southern end of the bridge. I remember feeling relief that we were staying put, as I never fancied river crossings. As the colonel was about to depart he beckoned Lieutenant Woods over to him for a few words.

The lieutenant had no sooner left us than the Scots sergeant told me that I was to go across the road to the Mortar Platoon house and bring back his small pack, which he had inadvertently left there. He gave me detailed instructions as to where it was to be found but I was not very happy about these proceedings as he was practically sentencing me to death for what seemed an almost frivolous reason. However, as the lieutenant was not there and it was a direct order from a superior there was nothing I could do but obey. He advised me to leave by one of the side windows as it would have been suicidal to go out of the front door, then to head for our gun pits in the centre of the island. Here I could pause briefly before making the final dash to the Mortar Platoon house.

He gave me a hand out of the window, which was about six feet above the pavement. Directly below me was a dead German soldier and I was forced to use his corpse as a rather gruesome stepping stone to the pavement. My heel-plates clinked against the metal badges that covered his chest, indicating that he was a veteran of many campaigns.

I went back down the side road about twenty yards, my idea being to start my run from there to work up a good turn of speed before flashing into the sights of some over-keen enemy machine gunner. Being a fast runner, even with battle order on, I was going a fair lick when I burst from cover into the main street, but was only halfway to the island when Jerry, who had the whole area sewn up by this time, opened fire with an MG34. My legs seemed to turn to water, for the rate of fire was so rapid that it appeared as if the bullets were tearing up the ground behind me faster than I could possibly run.

One last spurt sent me sprawling on top of an astonished mortar crew, who looked at me as though I were a visitor from another planet. Willing hands lowered me into a position of comparative safety. The four mortar men were sitting quite calmly, each on a pile of ten-pound mortar bombs. From somewhere they had 'liberated' a magnificent tea service and a cuppa was thrust into my trembling hands, which someone held steady while I drank the hot sweet reviving liquid.

'Where the hell are you going, Kid?' asked one of them. 'Over to the house to get Sergeant Mac's small pack,' I replied. 'The Scotch bastard, why didn't he go himself?' The pit was overcrowded, so after my drink I decided to push on. Four pairs of brawny arms sent me staggering on my way. This added momentum carried me to the shelter of the side street by the Mortar Platoon house, where I was able to draw breath. A door led into the back garden, which was deserted. A sentry challenged me from the house and then removed just enough barrier material for me to squeeze through. It looked as though the back kitchen was on fire but a closer inspection revealed innumerable tommy cookers set up just anywhere and going full blast. No one seemed interested in my arrival as they were all too busy brewing up or cooking. Unlike the barren White House that I had so recently left, this place was simply bursting with preserved foods, sweets, chocolates and drink of all kinds. I reported to Sergeant Jackman, the Platoon Sergeant, who helped me find the Scots sergeant's pack. As things seemed to be hotting up I decided to return to the White House straight away.

Outside, Jerry was putting down a really terrific mortar barrage. I made for the slit-trench that Slapsie and I had shared together. The morning now seemed an eternity ago and there was no sign of Slapsie, who must have been recalled to the house. Indeed, apart from the two gun crews, the island was almost deserted. An MG34 lashed out at a target down the road behind me, the tracer showing up vividly against the gathering dusk. Despite the heavy machine-gun fire Sergeant Hamilton materialised out of the darkness and proceeded to give me a good dressing-down. Evidently he was under the impression that I had been hiding in the relative comfort of the Mortar Platoon house all day. Vainly I tried to explain where I had come from and where I intended to go as soon as I could summon up enough courage to leave the slit-trench. I was rather surprised and hurt that he didn't seem to know that I had been with Lieutenant Woods since early in the morning; but with lead flying in every direction the sergeant was not inclined to be reasonable. He gave me a direct order to stay where I was or be shot. As far as I was concerned that was the end of the matter. In the Army you always obeyed the last order. In the long run this order of Joe's probably saved my life.

As evening fell enemy activity subsided but our lads came to life; out went the riflemen, cocky and confident, looking for Jerry. At night we had moral, if not material, superiority. Of course it was never pitch black, as there were so many fires from blazing enemy tanks and trucks, while some of the houses were alight as well. This sudden flickering light could be most confusing and there were nervy bursts of machine-gun fire from trigger-happy Germans who saw British paratroopers in every shadow.

The second night in Arnhem and no relief yet. Could we possibly hold out until midday on Tuesday? From the surrounding street, held by the enemy, came the ominous sound of tank engines. Jerry was getting ready for the third day.

Chapter 5

HOLD ON!

———

TUESDAY 19 September opened with the roar of powerful German armoured car engines revving up along the road to the west by which we had entered Arnhem. It was like the start of a Grand Prix and one could almost imagine the enemy drivers jockeying for a favourable position. Some damned fool must have dropped the starting flag because they came tearing down the road towards our island, their machine guns going full blast, raking our position with fire. However, this was largely ineffectual because there were so few paratroopers still remaining in the open and those few had dug themselves well in. Once again from the comfortable depths of the slit-trench I heard the familiar words of command ring out from the airborne anti-tank gunners. Though completely without cover these magnificent men brought their 6-pounders into action and the leading armoured car ground to a flaming halt, while those that followed either piled into it or fell victim to the heavy fire that poured from the airborne-held houses. What was left of the German team beat a hasty retreat.

I raised my head but a burst of extremely malicious machine-gun fire kicked sand in my face and I subsided to the bottom of the trench again. Despite the fact that we had won every action that had developed, the pressure was now on and Jerry had us pinned down. Although his losses as the attacker were heavier than ours, we had received no reinforcements since the battle commenced, and we were losing men rapidly as he maintained his attack. We asked ourselves again what had happened to the remainder of the 1st Airborne Division which was supposed to have dropped the day before. What had become of the Polish Para Brigade? Where was the Second Army? It was true that this latest enemy attack from the west had been stopped, but it had been in strength and from the very direction we were expecting relief. It now looked as though only about half the 2nd Battalion and some supporting troops had ever reached Arnhem. And where was all the German armour coming from? Events so far had been very different from what we had been led to expect.

After the failure of the 'Grand Prix' attack the Germans withdrew a short distance and began to mortar and shell our positions systematically for the first time. The very air seemed to wail and sigh with the number of projectiles passing through it. The enemy had also brought up some self-propelled artillery, heavy stuff, and against this we were virtually helpless. One by one the houses held by the paratroopers were set alight. There was nothing to fight the fires with, even if we had been able to. The airborne soldiers kept on firing from the blazing buildings even with the roof fallen in; then they moved to the second floor, then to the first, and finally to the basement. Only when this was alight did they evacuate the building and take over another. As each hour passed we were driven into a smaller and smaller area. Casualties began to mount rapidly. Our food and water were practically gone, but worst of all the ammunition was running short.

Soon we heard tank engines and thought at first they were ours; but they were German panzers cautiously probing their way into the bloody arena to add the sharp crack of their 75 and 88mm guns to the already overwhelming bombardment.

It seemed impossible that the shelling and mortaring could get any worse, but they did. The separate explosions now merged into one almost-continuous rolling detonation and the earth shook as if it was alive. My head sang and I was numb to any feeling beyond the basic instinct to survive. I began to realise the full significance of the phrase 'bomb-happy'. Yet even in this terrific concentration of fire not one bomb or shell splinter landed in a slit-trench or mortar pit: it was unbelievable, little short of miraculous. It is only when one has been through this sort of experience that one can understand how soldiers in the past stood in lines facing each other and fired by numbers.

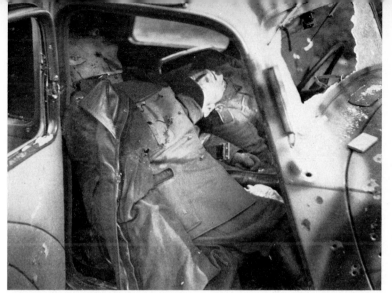

Major-General Kussin, *Stadtkommandant* of Arnhem, lying dead in his car after it had been ambushed by British paratroopers on 17 September 1944. *See Page 39* BU 1154

RAF photograph of the northern ramp of the Arnhem bridge, 18 September 1944. The wreckage is the remains of a German armoured column which had tried to rush the bridge from the south MH 2062

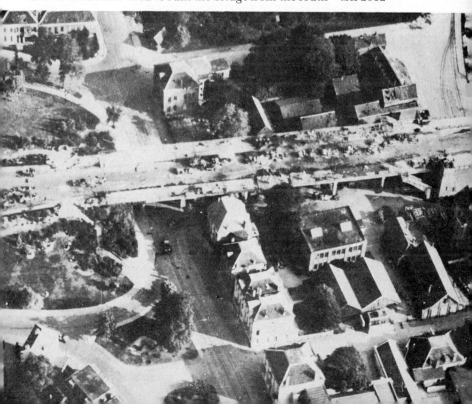

German photograph of dead British paratroopers   HU 2135

3-inch mortar crew in action during the battle of Arnhem   BU 1099

A *Sturmgeschütz* III 75mm self-propelled gun belonging to the 9th
SS Panzer Division in a street in Arnhem. Note the dimpled surface
of the vehicle, a treatment designed to prevent magnetic mines and
grenades adhering to the hull and turret   *Bundesarchiv, Koblenz*

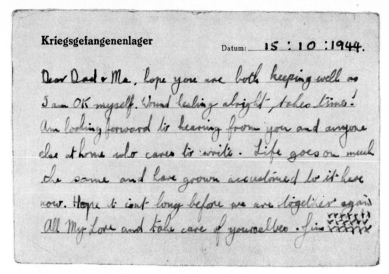

Kriegsgefangenenlager   Datum: 15 : 10 : 1944.

Dear Dad & Ma, hope you are both keeping well as I am OK myself. Wound healing alright, takes time! Am looking forward to hearing from you and anyone else at home who cares to write. Life goes on much the same and have grown accustomed to it here now. Hope it isn't long before we are together again. All my love and take care of yourselves . Jim ✗✗✗✗✗

Postcard sent by the author from Stalag XIB to his parents in Brighton, 15 October 1944   HU 28876

The author's CO, Lieutenant-Colonel (now Major-General) John Frost, addressing survivors in Arnhem on the occasion of the unveiling of a memorial to those who fell at the bridge, September 1945   HU 33302

With each successive salvo of mortar bombs I screwed my steel helmet further into the comforting earth and clawed at the silty soil at the bottom of the trench. I kept repeating to myself over and over again, 'Hold on . . . hold on . . . you must hold on.'

To be alone at the bottom of that trench was like lying in a newly dug grave waiting to be buried alive. Each fresh explosion sent rivulets of earth crumbling around my helmet and into the sides of my mouth. After another avalanche of explosions I started praying, and really meaning it, for the first time in my life.

Overhead a lone Messerschmitt fighter plane circled lazily. If the pilot was spotting for the enemy artillery he had an almost impossible task as the Germans and ourselves were so close together, even sharing the same houses in some cases. Perhaps he was just curious – it was certainly the only aircraft I saw throughout the battle. What had happened to the mighty Allied air forces God only knew.

Something whistled down into the slit-trench and hit my boot. In one split second I suffered agonies visualising extinction, but as nothing happened I gingerly reached towards my ankle and retrieved the tail fin of a German mortar bomb, still warm from flight. It must have been blown into my trench from an exploding missile nearby.

The bombardment suddenly ceased and there was an uncanny quiet, which was abruptly shattered by the eruption of an enemy infantry attack from underneath the bridge directly in front of our positions. This desperate assault came to nothing and those not cut down fled in disorder.

One German soldier fell just outside the White House. Two airborne medics carrying a stretcher ran out from our battalion headquarters building to aid him. Both stretcher bearers were unarmed and wore armbands bearing the Red Cross symbol. They also had large red crosses on a white disc on both sides of their helmets, and their mission must have been obvious to everyone. We were horrified to hear the ripping fire of a German machine gun and to see the front man crumple into the gutter. The man at the rear of the stretcher was so astonished at what had happened that for a second or two he just stood still holding the stretcher's rear handles before dropping them and sprinting for his life. A hail of bullets followed his progress but at last he made it to safety.

A howl of rage went up from the watching paratroopers at this act of murder. The body of the dead orderly lay not more than ten yards from me. His eyes were closed and from the peaceful expression on his face one might almost have thought that he had fallen asleep in that gutter. Alongside him his steel helmet, marked with the cross of mercy, rocked gently to a standstill, making a noise that sounded like 'lunka, lunka, lunka, lunka, lunka' over and over again until it stopped. The German wounded outside the White House appeared to have succumbed and there they lay together, enemies a few minutes before, now united in death. Debris from the house fell on them, completely burying the Germans and falling across the legs and back of the murdered medic. Bits of the debris were on fire. The flames got hold of the uniform of the medic and licked hungrily along his spine. I looked away.

Now death stalked the streets round the northern end of the road bridge. It lurked in the pall of thick black smoke that hung over us; it kept watch in the gardens and streets for the unwary and cut them down. It was nearly noon on Tuesday 19 September and there was still no sign of relief. A shout from one of the windows of the Mortar Platoon house caught my attention. 'Blimey, there's someone still down there. Eh, you! Come on inside out of it.' 'But Joe told me to stay here,' I shouted. 'There's no one else out there except you,' said the voice. 'Come on in!'

The last one left on the island! How had I been overlooked when everyone else had been recalled? Probably because I was so far down in that slit-trench that everyone thought it was empty.

Gathering my gear and rifle together I slid out of the trench and made once again for the rear entrance of the Mortar Platoon house. As I did so there rang out a fusillade of shots, one of which hit my small pack and spun it round by my side. I reached the rear entrance without further incident, but getting back into the building was no longer such a casual process. More men were guarding the barricaded rear of the building and were

obviously preparing for whatever Jerry had in mind next. Outside the house it was pretty quiet, although from nearby streets
one could hear the clatter of steel tracks and the snorting roar of
tank engines.

There was a telephone in the hall of the house. As I went past
it started to ring. Automatically I reached for the receiver but
my wrist was seized by Sergeant Smith, a tough jovial man
from one of the other sections. 'That's Jerry ringing up, but the
lady of the house isn't at home. Got it?'

The platoon was being organised to defend the house as riflemen now that our two mortars were out of action through lack
of ammunition – the island was untenable anyway. Such men
as could be spared either rested or cooked what was left of
the grub for the men manning the doors and windows. The
Germans had very considerately cut off the water supply but
this did not prove a hardship in this house because of the large
supply of wines and spirits. No one had called to disconnect the
telephone and there was already a story going around that one
of our lads had got through to the Arnhem exchange and asked
to be connected to a Mr Winston Churchill in Downing Street,
London.

Another story was that when a German patrol had entered
one of the gardens a paratrooper had rung up the local police
station to complain of 'intruders'. Well, these stories could have
been true, they were typical of the rather hearty humour of airborne types. Everyone seemed cheerful and there was no des-
pondency. One chap called Cook was actually sitting on the
stairs strumming a banjo. The enemy started shelling again. A
para jerked his head in the direction of the banjo player and
remarked, 'You can hardly blame them!'

Sergeant Jackman told me to familarise myself with the layout
of the house and try to make myself generally useful. Looking
round someone else's home is fascinating, especially when you
can open drawers and cupboards as though you were a detective
hunting for clues. From the large crucifix on the wall and the
unusual number of medallions and rosaries to be found, the
previous occupants must have been Roman Catholics. They had
also been ardent Nazis, judging by the amount of anti-Jewish

literature to be found. One such pamphlet was *De Joden in Nederland*, which I kept as a souvenir.

There was a desk which had been broken open and rifled, and piles of letters lay scattered about. They had nearly all originated from South America but as they were written in Spanish there was no way of telling if they were in any way connected with the National Socialist movement. There was a collection of match-box tops, together with stamps, more medallions and coins. I found a really beautiful rosary, which I decided to take back to a Catholic friend, and I also pinched a small goat made of silver, standing on a circular plate studded with daisies.

By this time most of the furniture in the house had been broken up to be used for barricades and consequently the floors were littered with clothing. Some of this, including sheets and curtains, had been made into couches, which had been placed behind the barricaded windows for those on watch to lie on. The owners of the house must have been well off, for the materials were superior to anything I had ever seen. As Max Miller would have said, 'All good stuff, lady – no rubbish.'

All the windows had been smashed out to provide a good field of fire. I went upstairs into one of the rear rooms which over-looked the back garden. I could only see out of the top of the window because a large wardrobe had been pulled in front of it. Down the side-road from which I had entered the garden a battle was going on between airborne and German patrols. Shots, screams, the explosion of hand grenades and the chatter-ing of automatic weapons drifted up. Through the small area of window available I saw the tower of a nearby church. It had a large clock-face, and was being shelled by the enemy under the mistaken assumption that we were using it as an observation post. Every shot that hit the tower sent the hands of the clock spinning round as though time itself was anxious to get the matter settled once and for all.

The sergeants seldom looked now at their coveted luminous-dialled service wrist-watches. I wondered if they realised that each section kept a list showing who would inherit the watch if the sergeant was killed. If a sergeant 'bought it' the watch was, of course, officially written-off, especially in an action such as this, but the lads made arrangements to pass it on according to rank and length of service. Guess who was bottom on our section sergeant's watch list.

I sat down on a bed from which the mattresses had been removed and took off my steel helmet for the first time in nearly three days. Fifty hours had passed and yet there was still no sign of the Second Army. It looked as though something had gone terribly wrong. I rested my head in my hands for a moment or two. Then I replaced my helmet and wandered into one of the front bedrooms which overlooked the island and the north-western end of the bridge. The familiar black clouds of smoke hung over the whole area and the stench of burning debris and expended cordite was overpowering. One of the defenders, who was lying prone behind a window, told me to get down. 'There's no one out there,' I whispered. In reply he nodded to a still figure lying in one corner. 'That's what *he* thought.'

Although the shattered face was mercifully covered by a bloodstained rag I recognised the corpse by the tight black curly hair and the huge frame. As I looked down on the body it hardly seemed a couple of weeks ago that he had come up to me in the middle of Grantham and asked me if I could write. When he found out that I could he took me into a nearby haberdashers and we borrowed a scratchy old pen and a dusty bottle of ink from a scared young girl assistant wearing the standard uniform of drab black dress and white collar. Then the giant asked me to complete a sleeping-out pass that he had liberated from some adjutant's desk so that he could stay the night with a girl in Nottingham. I duly obliged. Now he was asleep for good, dreaming, one could only hope, of the beer and beautiful girls of Nottingham – he would never need another sleeping-out pass.

'Did you hear about Slapsie?' someone asked. 'No,' I replied, going cold. 'Is he wounded?' 'He's dead.' 'God! When?' 'This morning. Walked past one of the windows and they spotted him from the bridge. Cannon shell. Nearly blew him in half.'

Slapsie dead! I was stunned – it was hardly possible. To me he had always seemed indestructible. The Old Soldier, the ex-Commando, the veteran of Narvik, Tunisia, Sicily and Italy, dead! He had been a real character, with the rough and ready humour of London's East End. We had shared the same billet, eaten together, drunk together, taken the mickey out of each other, and mucked in together on training schemes and in action. Now he was gone. There would be no more bagpiped cats or bombs that lit up in your face. By the very reason of his open nature and robust sense of humour his death cast a cloud over all of us. I was shaken. While making my way downstairs I ran into Sergeant Smith, who took one look at me and gave me a bottle of Cherry Brandy to have a swig from.

I was really grateful for this and must still have been under the influence of the brandy's warming glow when Sergeant Jackman asked for a volunteer to venture out to the island to recover a Bren gun left behind there and now badly needed. I stepped forward. The effect of the alcohol quickly evaporated as we made our way to the front door and took down the barricade. Sergeant Jackman reckoned that although the way out through the back garden and side gate was perhaps the safer, the enemy would not expect anyone to emerge from the front entrance. Another factor was that the distance was halved in this way. We half opened the door and peered out. The island did indeed look ridiculously close, perhaps about ten yards.

The sergeant smiled reassuringly and said, 'OK. It looks quiet. Make a dash for it and I'll cover you.' I shot forward before I started to think about what I was doing, made for the trench nearest the Bren gun and rolled into it. I pulled the gun into the trench but there was no magazine. 'OK. Come in!' called the sergeant. I doubled back carrying the emasculated LMG. Sergeant Jackman was naturally disappointed that I couldn't find a magazine and I rather half-heartedly offered to go back to the island again, but as we had got away with it once he decided not to tempt fate again. Mumbling that he would rustle up a magazine from one of the adjoining houses he sent me upstairs to relieve one of the men there.

Dusk was falling, although there was so much smoke about from the many fires near the bridge that it already seemed quite dark. Smoke partly obscured the White House, now well alight although still defended by paratroopers and engineers. The roof of the Mortar Platoon house was also on fire; every now and then a large chunk of burning wood or other debris would fall with a shuddering crash into the street. Every time there was a direct hit or near-explosion clouds of white plaster dust came down, covering our uniforms and faces, blinding and choking us. On the bridge we could hear the noise of tank engines and for a moment had hopes that it might be our relieving force, hopes that were shattered as we recognised the monstrous SS-manned Tiger tanks, which were trying to bulldoze their way past the still-burning enemy armour blocking the road. Behind the Tigers we could dimly make out more German armour creeping forward under the steel umbrella provided by the girders of the bridge. Experience had made the Germans cautious, though by this time we had nothing with which to oppose them but hand grenades of one type or another.

It seemed that we had had it. The great thrust by the Second Army to join up with us had failed. We felt bitter and betrayed. We didn't speak much but I well remember saying, 'I wonder what it's going to be like to die.' To which one of the veterans replied with a grin, 'Don't know, Kid. Never tried it.'

I lay on my couch of coats, squinting down the barrel of my rifle at the smoke and flickering fires. A large box of chocolate liqueurs lay between me and another para. My fingers caressed silken cloth and I wondered if they would ever feel the soft skin of a girl again. My chin rested on my rifle butt and my helmet was tilted well forward over my eyes: I was terrified of being blinded. As I munched the rich Dutch chocolates I pondered on my fate, thinking of the seeming inevitability of death and that, at nineteen, I had seen so very little of life.

A wild-eyed soldier burst into the room. 'If any of you have taken rosaries from this house get rid of them,' he blurted out. When we asked why he replied, 'Every one of our blokes who has copped it has been found with a rosary clasped in his hand.' He rushed out leaving us gaping after him, but the para next to me laughed and muttered softly, 'Daft bastard!' This was one of the few times I heard anyone swear in the last hours. It was as though my comrades grew in stature and all the small irritating quirks of character disappeared. Ennobled in some strange way by this physical and spiritual auto-da-fe, each man appeared concerned for his neighbour rather than for himself. All seemed prepared for the end and ready to face it. The word 'surrender' was not mentioned and I doubt if it had even been thought of.

A burst of enemy tracer from the northern road behind us ribboned its way over the White House. This was Jerry's warning that he was about to shell the building, so the occupants had better get out. The reply was a burst of Bren-gun fire. Down the northern road, to our left but out of sight, we could plainly hear the guttural German commands and the slam of the breech block as the shell was loaded into the barrel of a self-propelled gun. The enemy gave the paratroopers about five minutes to surrender, but when no one emerged the order to fire was given.

The first shell burst against the White House at a range of something under a hundred yards. It hit a top storey near the roof and the entire building seemed to shake itself like a dog. We could plainly see the riflemen and airborne engineers, caution thrown to the winds, kneeling openly inside the blasted windows, pouring fire down at the Germans as though determined to take as many as possible with them to death. This fire had no effect on the heavily armoured SP gun, which crept nearer. Once again we heard the command to load. Since our arrival on Sunday the houses and warehouses in our occupation had received terrific punishment, especially the White House, but it still looked, even with its roof on fire, an impregnable fortress. The German SP crashed out and a second shell hit the White House.

We watched in horrified silence as the walls appeared to breathe out before the whole structure collapsed. The roof and floors fell inside and a towering column of flame shot into the sky. A cut-off scream marked the end of many gallant riflemen and engineers. The sudden collapse of such a solid-looking edifice was a terrific shock to our morale, and when we heard the SP growling around in the street as it moved position we held our breath. A stream of tracer lashed out over our house, at which we all jumped to our feet and turned towards the door – only to find Sergeant Jackman standing there grinning at us. 'Just where do you lot think you're off to?'

The panic subsided, but when the sergeant ordered us downstairs at the double we needed no second bidding. The remainder of the Mortar Platoon was clustered at the bottom of the stairs. From above Sergeants Jackman and Kalikoff surveyed what was left of the original 'shower'. Sergeant Jackman was now in command of the platoon, Lieutenant Woods being presumed killed in the White House.

Having inspected us Sergeant Jackman said, 'I want six volunteers to stay here with Maurice and defend this house to the last.' We all shuffled forward. 'OK, Maurice, take your pick.' Sergeant Kalikoff looked us over in his sad way and selected six of the toughest veterans in the room. Waving his hand in the direction of the garden Sergeant Jackman shouted, 'Right, the rest outside and dig in.'

We tumbled out of the house and spread round the perimeter of the garden. I selected a spot near the west wall by a large tree. One of my comrades handed me a pick with the words, 'Get cracking, the big stuff'll be falling soon.'

All that was left of the Mortar Platoon commenced to dig in while in the adjoining garden HQ Company was doing the same. The Germans resumed their bombardment as they didn't relish coming in themselves to try to take our positions. I had just removed my small pack, placed my rifle against the wall and raised my pick to make the first strike when there was a deafening explosion. A blast of hot air hit me in the back and at the same time a burst of shrapnel tore into my left leg. The stench of expended cordite and smoke was overpowering but somehow I was still on my feet. My leg suddenly went numb and my head seemed swollen to twice its normal size, my brain continuing to function in a detached sort of way. It took a tremendous effort to lower the pick from my shoulder to the ground, where I used it to steady myself. From behind me came moans and then a cry, 'Jesus Christ! I'm blind, I'm blind! Help me!'

Recognising the voice as that of an Irish member of the platoon I tried to turn, and called out, 'OK Paddy, I'm coming. Hold on!' I managed to twist myself round so that I could see him. He was holding his hands over his face as he collapsed into a half-scooped-out slit-trench. Several others lay about, their bodies distorted by the explosion; all seemed to be dead. They had caught the full fury of the shell whereas I had merely received the backlash. As I took a pace towards the Irishman the garden started to spin, and I fell backwards as a great darkness claimed me.

Chapter 6

ESCAPE FROM VALHALLA

THE WORLD was a red glow smelling of smoke and death. From far away came the sound of voices. Shells exploded in the garden and splinters of steel cut through the branches of the trees overhead. Through the red haze two figures appeared, airborne medics, who knelt down and spoke softly and reassuringly to me in the manner of the whole to the wounded. 'Hang on, old lad, we'll soon have you out of this.'

Two sets of brawny arms hauled me upright. The two men hooked my arms round their necks, and we hustled to the end of the garden with my dead weight sagging between them. I was conscious of my feet attempting to keep pace with the rest of my body as it was dragged along. A shell exploded against a wall on our left and the blast brought us down; but none of the sighing splinters hit us – another miracle.

We continued on through a wooden gate and down a path leading to the rear entrance of the Headquarters building. It appeared to be crammed with paratroops and there were great comings and goings. Morale was extremely high and men winked at me and shouted encouragement as I was borne below ground to the cellars where the wounded were being cared for. These had been turned into a makeshift hospital run by Captain Logan, our Scots medical officer, and his devoted team of medical orderlies.

The scene was a grim one. The floors were carpeted with dead and badly wounded airborne soldiers, more and more of whom were being brought in every minute. Many of the Royal Army Medical Corps orderlies had already been killed attempting to rescue the wounded; consequently the survivors of this brave band of men were out on their feet with exhaustion. The two medics set me down on a table in the centre of the room adjoining the cellars and reported my arrival to Captain Logan, who was busy with another of the wounded. He straightened up, came over and examined me. His eyes were lost in deep sockets and his face was haggard from lack of sleep, yet his voice was quiet and sympathetic, his hands capable yet gentle.

The wound was cleaned and I was given an injection while an orderly scribbled details of my treatment on a tie-on label which he attached to my camouflage jacket. I tried to sit up to look at the wound. The medics had cut my battledress trouser leg from just above the web gaiter to below the hip, the bloodstained remnant being removed. My fingers groped gingerly towards the numb area inside my left thigh where a large carnation of shattered flesh erupted just above the knee. There were also two holes at the back of the knee and another wound at the back of the calf. As Captain Logan applied a shell dressing he seemed to recede from me with astonishing rapidity and I passed out.

When I came to I found myself in a very small vault off the main cellar. It must have been some sort of archway because my head and feet nearly touched the brick. There was no direct illumination, only a ghastly half-light which filtered in from the main cellar. I lay between two other soldiers. A medic leaned over one of them and asked me how I felt and if I'd like a cup of tea. He half-filled a mess tin with what looked like hot brown water. I enquired how things were going. 'Pretty grim,' he told me. 'The army doesn't seem able to make it.'

He said that two hours had elapsed since I had been brought in. He leaned over the body of an officer who lay on my right: 'H'm, this poor blighter's nearly had it.' The officer was strapped up with towels and bandages but still the blood seeped out of him on to the floor. He looked as though he had been riddled with machine-gun bullets, and he muttered incessantly, apparently re-living his last patrol. This always ended with a shouted warning, 'Look out, Peter!' Then he seemed to be at home again and was talking to his wife and children, after which he returned to the patrol, always ending with that shouted warning to Peter, probably a fellow officer. As he switched from one conversation to another, from Arnhem to home and back again, his words were exactly the same. It was like listening to a gramophone record when the needle has stuck.

The orderly stood up and shook his head. 'Poor devil, only a matter of time now.' He stepped over and bent down by a still figure on the other side of me. 'How are you, matey?' he said. 'Like a drink?'

There was no reply, for the man's face had been completely shot away. A shell dressing covered what had been his eyes and nose, and a large piece of gauze mercifully veiled what had once been his jaws. A slight movement of the head and a bubbling sound from the gauze told me that this shell-torn fragment of humanity was still alive. The orderly got a cup of water and what looked like a fountain pen filler, a sort of glass stem with a rubber ball on the top. He filled the glass tube with water and spoke to the faceless paratrooper as he held his right hand. 'Now, matey, I'm going to give you a drink of water. OK?' A slight pressure from the man's hand told him that he had understood and the orderly began to drip water on to the gauze where the mouth should have been, a drop at a time. Each drop must have taken minutes to filter through the gauze but the orderly seemed to possess endless patience.

The dying officer rambled on; even in the last few minutes his voice had grown noticeably weaker. The thick cellar walls deadened the sounds of the battle raging outside, but every now and again came the ominous rumble of falling masonry. Each successive concussion covered us from head to foot in dust. Eventually this building too would collapse, and then what would become of us?

'I've got to go now,' said the medic, 'try to get some shut-eye.' As he disappeared I took stock of my situation. I was wounded and losing blood, and surrounded by dying men in a building already ablaze. My mind drifted off and I was a child again in Sheffield. How I had hated school! But I liked the stories we were told about the Black Forest where lived a sinister dwarf by the name of Schwartz:

> Clang, clang, clang on the anvil
> In the smithy by the dark North Sea.

Is it Thor who is striking with his hammer?
Is it Odin with the leather on his knee?
Clang, clang, clang on the anvil
There are steel ships wanted on the sea.
  Clang, clang, clang on the anvil
And the flames of the forge run deep:
Old Thor with his hammer glowing
Had his eyes on the furrows of the deep.
Clang, clang, clang on the anvil
For the sword, the sword of the mighty will not sleep.

Wild dreams troubled my fitful sleep. I found myself walking over uneven ground amid swirling mists. Figures appeared on each side of me but vanished when I spoke to them. I came to a flight of stone steps leading up to two huge doors made of heavy beams of wood bound with iron. Two immense iron rings opened them. From behind the doors came the sound of many voices and, eager for human company, I seized one of the rings and pushed the door open. A huge hall stretched before me into infinity. On the lofty walls inside hung circular shields and spears. Soldiers of every nationality sat at long trestle tables, all talking at once; the scene resembled a mammoth regimental reunion, and the noise was like the constant roar of an incoming sea. As each in turn tried to outdo the others in recounting some vivid experience in battle, they drank from tankards which were constantly refilled by tall fair girls of unearthly beauty whom, strangely enough, the soldiers seemed to disregard. Three men rose from one of the tables. With a thrill of horror I recognised them as three of my comrades who had been killed in battle.

They called to me. 'Thought you'd never get here.' 'What took you so long?' 'You're safe now. It's all over for you.' I backed towards the door and my three comrades stopped and looked at me. One stepped forward and held out his hand. 'Come and sit down. Don't go back.' All the soldiers were silent and the blondes held their pitchers still. Everyone was looking at me with anticipation. The spell broke as my dead comrade took another step towards me. With a shriek I turned and fled from the hall back into the grey mist, while behind me the dead warriors cried, 'Come back! Come back!' I stumbled over the broken ground babbling in terror and woke to find the medic shaking me back to reality.

'You OK, matey? Blimey, you weren't half creating.' He knelt and grabbed me under the arms. 'Let's have you out of this lot.' Gently he lifted me from the floor where I was lying in the congealed blood of the now-dead officer. As he did so there was a sound like the removal of adhesive plaster from flesh. He pulled me across the body of the faceless one, also mercifully dead, to take my chance in the main cellar with those wounded still alive.

'What day is it?' I asked. 'Wednesday the twentieth,' was the reply. 'Any sign of the army?' 'No. Looks like we've had it.' However, things didn't seem too bad: we were still holding out and I was alive.

This more spacious cellar was illuminated by the daylight coming in through two smaller windows set high up, and it was better ventilated than the vault had been. A number of ledgers had been removed from their wooden storage racks. They were so large, about six feet by three when opened, that there was room for a grown man to lie on them. They served as beds and at least kept us off the ice-cold concrete floor. They were the biggest books I had ever seen, and I couldn't help thinking of all the painstaking work that had gone into the compilation of those columns of neatly written figures, records of the transactions of some sound Arnhem merchant. Now their beautiful entries were stained by the blood of the paratroopers, and soon they and the building would be destroyed. What a waste of effort it all seemed, and yet it was as nothing compared with the human waste going on in the surrounding street.

I still felt very faint but far more cheerful, for the wounded who were brought into my part of the cellar were very much alive. They joked, cursed and shouted to one another, passing on first-hand reports of the battle as these were relayed downstairs by the handful of men above who were still holding out. Food, water and ammunition were nearly all gone and the men still fighting had been down to collect the bullets and grenades in the possession of the dead and wounded. Despite our situation no one complained and the only moans came from those seriously wounded and in great pain.

By this time, as far as we knew, this building was the only one still held by the paratroopers. Even though it was well on fire there was no talk of surrender. We still clung to the hope of an eleventh-hour miracle, trusting that our sacrifice was not to be in vain.

The day passed, punctuated by explosions, machine-gun fire and the sounds of boots and voices outside the window. Sometimes the voices were German, sometimes British, as the yard outside changed hands again and again. The increased shelling began to have a very bad effect on the wounded, but they stuck it well although we were all smothered in brick dust. We were told that a Tiger tank was now right outside the building with its gun muzzle practically in the front entrance. As though in confirmation there were terrific explosions upstairs. The smell of burning and the thick smoke got steadily worse and the number of wounded continued to grow by the minute.

The wounded were now so tightly packed in the cellar that it was almost impossible for the orderlies to step between them. I wanted to relieve myself and had to ask for assistance. An orderly half carried and half dragged me upstairs past defenders who were still firing at the enemy out of holes in the wall or through shattered windows. Some of them were slightly wounded but they turned and grinned at me, shouting encouragement and items of news and making ribald jokes at my expense. We reached the WC, which was in a 'worse state than Russia', choked up and really filthy. I couldn't help smiling when I reflected that with my leg shot-up, trapped in a building on fire and surrounded by Hitler's élite SS panzers, all I was upset about was a bunged-up lavatory pan.

On the way back I noticed that several paratroopers were counting their rounds of ammo. One man had only a clip of five left. At the foot of the stairs airborne signallers had set up a powerful radio transmitter and were in touch with Second Army. A major wearing the grey beret and spearhead badge of the Reconnaissance Corps was talking earnestly into a hand microphone: 'We cannot hold out much longer. Our position is desperate. Please hurry.'

He repeated the message over and over again. I learned that, Colonel Frost having been wounded, this recce major was now in command of all that remained of those troops who had reached the road bridge.

Back in the cellar morale was still high and everyone bombarded me with questions as to what was happening. The second-in-command of HQ Company came down and received the same reception. 'How are we doing, sir?' 'Where's the Second Army?' 'How's the ammo lasting out?' 'Have we got a chance, sir?'

Although the questions were shouted, it was in a respectful manner to a man whose physical resemblance to a great German soldier had earned him the nickname 'Rommel'. The major told us we were doing very well but that time was against us, and he asked if anyone had any grenades or bullets left for the men still fighting. He also informed us that the infantry of a famous old county regiment belonging to XXX Corps had actually got across the Rhine just outside the town. At the time I thought he was just telling us this to raise our spirits, but I later discovered it was true. Unfortunately, these brave men of the Dorsets ended up in the Stalag with us.

The major also told us that he had already knocked out four enemy tanks and was just off to bag another. Minutes later we heard that he had been killed in the attempt, the end of a first-class officer.

The afternoon wore on and we dozed or rambled away, each in his separate delirium. One minute I was at home with my parents, the next at Grantham; then I was in action on a seemingly non-stop roller coaster of feverish dreams.

By 4 pm it was obvious that our position was hopeless. We could plainly hear the crackle of burning wood upstairs and it was becoming painful to breathe because of the dense smoke. Some action had to be taken if we were not to be suffocated or burned to death. Colonel Frost gave the order for the few gallant men still holding the Germans at bay and the walking wounded, who included several blinded paras roped together, to make a break for it and leave the rest of us to our fate. This was the only possible decision under the circumstances but was not too well received by some of the more desperately wounded men. In their panic they tried to drag themselves upstairs, sobbing that they had been abandoned, forgetting that their commanding officer was lying among them.

Their fears were somewhat allayed by a medical officer who shouted, 'Don't worry lads. I'll get you out of here, even if I have to carry you all out myself. OK?' There was a rumble of approval as he continued, 'Now I shall try to contact the German commander.'

We heard him walk upstairs and step outside into the yard, calling out 'Cease fire!' A burst of enemy machine-gun fire sent him tumbling back inside again and we chuckled as we heard him describe the Germans in most unprofessional language. Then he had a brainwave and shouted in German for a cease-fire. At once the firing stopped and we heard the heavy tread of boots entering the yard, the hobnailed jackboots of the enemy. We could hear our medical officer rapidly explaining our plight to a German officer in English and stressing the urgency of removing us as soon as possible from the burning building, which was in imminent danger of collapse. Then came the sound of boots approaching the top of the stairs and starting to descend.

Suddenly a badly wounded paratrooper uncovered a Sten gun he had kept hidden ready to blast the Germans as they appeared. He was quickly overpowered by the equally badly wounded men on either side of him. He sobbed furiously over this and was quite fanatical in his hatred; but the deaths of the first two Germans who ventured down the stairs would have been a poor exchange for all the wounded airborne soldiers in the cellar. After such a reception the enemy would have been quite justified in slinging grenades down among us, which, in such overcrowding, would have resulted in the most fearful carnage.

We did not know what to expect from Jerry and by this time many of us were past caring. My own feelings were relief that it was all over and also extreme curiosity regarding the enemy. The first to enter the cellar was an officer wearing a greatcoat and steel helmet. Round his neck hung an Iron Cross and a pair of field glasses, and in his right hand he carried an automatic carbine. He looked tired and drawn, and was obviously shocked by what he saw, his expression being one of total disbelief. He rapped out orders, which were instantly obeyed. More and more German troops appeared. They picked up the wounded with great care and began to clear the cellar. Fortunately we had fallen into the hands of the regular soldiers of the Wehrmacht and not, thank God, into the clutches of the SS.

A huge Canadian press photographer was in the cellar with us. He had already smashed his camera and plates. He lifted me as though I were a child and carried me upstairs. The ground floor was well ablaze and the whole building was about to cave in. As the Canadian stepped outside with me in his arms he had to jump to one side, for a massive piece of flaming timber hurtled down from the roof. Large chunks of brickwork and concrete were also coming down, adding to the danger of the evacuation.

There was a small courtyard in front of the building where an airborne 6-pounder anti-tank gun lay keeled over on its side. The barrel was smashed, one rubber tyre was burnt off and flames were licking the other. The entire gun crew lay spread-eagled where they had fallen amongst the tumbled cartridge cases. The scene resembled one of those oil paintings that you see in regimental museums entitled 'The Last Stand'. These air-borne gunners had nobly upheld the traditions of the Royal Regiment and their achievements were out of all proportion to their numbers.

The Canadian laid me down on a grass bank facing our former headquarters. It was amazing to see the change in the area during the past seventy-two hours. All the houses and ware-houses we had held were completely destroyed by fire. We heard a shout and turned round. Dug into the bank were two German machine gunners wearing camouflage smocks. They wanted us to move over so as not to obstruct their field of fire, and this we did. Other German soldiers now surrounded us and I was amazed to see that most of them carried British rifles and Sten guns: we always thought that their weapons, particularly the Schmeisser sub-machine gun, were very much superior to ours.

Our Scots RSM lay at the bottom of the bank singing at the top of his voice. A German soldier told him to be quiet and cocked his gun, but he was completely 'bomb happy' and thought he was having a sing-song in the mess back home. We mimed his condition to the German, who seemed to understand.

A German NCO stood in the street shouting something like 'Drei Kompagnie!' His men came scurrying like grey rats from nearby houses to form up and march off in impressive style. They tried to drive our vehicles away and we had a few laughs at their efforts, especially with the Jeep, which bucked all over the road like a mustang to the accompaniment of ribald shouts of 'Ride him, cowboy!'

A Bren gun carrier rattled out from the rear of one of the buildings and someone exclaimed, 'Blimey, it's George.' We all thought by the expert way in which it was driven that George Hines, our Mortar Platoon driver, was at the controls, but a quiet voice behind us said, 'I'm here with you.' It was George, wounded and a prisoner like the rest of us. We should not have been surprised at Jerry's skilful handling of the Bren carrier as a large number of them fell into his hands in 1940 when the BEF left them behind at Dunkirk.

From the cellar of a burning building next to the ruins of the White House came a burst of Bren-gun fire which scattered our guards in panic and very nearly hit us. 'Cease fire! British wounded!' we shouted, and the firing stopped; we wondered what lone gunner was still fighting on.

The Germans quickly re-formed around us but were decidedly trigger-happy after such an experience. Some were quite decent to us and one of the older men gave me some delicious hot coffee, a tremendous sacrifice in wartime Germany or occupied territory. A younger man handed me some sausage and biscuits from his own rations. A tough-looking German sauntered up with a huge grin on his face. He wore a very non-military coloured scarf round his neck and was swathed in belts of machine-gun ammunition. The left side of his tunic was covered with campaign ribbons and attractive metal badges. He spoke good English and told us that he had been in the fighting in Normandy against Montgomery.

When we remarked on the stubborn resistance put up by the German Army at Caen he was delighted. 'Yes, six weeks solid we had of it,' he beamed, 'then they sent me up here for a rest. Some rest!' However, it was obvious he was as pleased as Punch to be on the winning side again so late in the war.

It was decided to shift us further back into the town in case an attempt was made to rescue us and we were ordered to stand up. A stocky dark-visaged German took out his bayonet, thrust it into the top of a liberated tin of British condensed milk and took a swig. I tapped him on the shoulder and asked him for a drink. Although he was a most surly-looking individual he wiped the tin clean with his sleeve and handed it to me. A smiling German NCO approached and asked me if I would prefer a stretcher, but as all the stretcher cases were being carried down a road leading to the river I declined his offer, afraid lest I be dumped in the Rhine. I never did discover whether the Germans disposed of any of our wounded in this way but I was not taking any chances. Two other wounded paratroopers hung my arms round their necks and we struggled along under the northern end of the bridge and then down a road to the left. Now we were in what had been enemy-held territory and we were amazed at the large number of dead in the street.

It was a shocking sight but also grimly gratifying to the British wounded to see, after our own losses, some of the punishment we had meted out. Remarks were heard like 'Blimey, never knew we killed so many of the bastards,' 'Look, lads – a good German,' and 'We certainly gave them as good as they gave us.'

Those Germans who had come to their doorways to watch us pass were naturally somewhat incensed by these remarks and made threatening gestures at us, but our guards closed in and hurried us along. By this time I wasn't sure whether I was holding up my two helpers or they were holding me up. The going was extremely hard for wounded men and we were physically exhausted. I wondered which of our trio, all with teeth gritted, would collapse first.

We turned another left-hand corner. Here, outside a shop, the Germans had taken up the paving stones and dug in a wicked-looking dual-purpose cannon. The barrel swept in a 180 degree arc of fire a few inches above the pavement. This small feature testified to the thoroughness with which our enemies approached every military problem; our blokes would have left the gun on top of the pavement and surrounded it with some sort of barricade.

The road we turned into had trees down each side and under these, parked nose-to-tail, were never-ending lines of German Mark IV tanks. In the dusk it was a truly impressive sight. Seeing my wonder a young enemy soldier remarked, 'Yes, Tommy, these were for you in the morning if you had not surrendered.' Several of the German tank men called out to us 'Well fought, Tommy,' 'Good fight, eh Tommy?' They seemed to regard war in much the same way as the British regarded football.

We turned into a cul-de-sac where the fit and the wounded were separated, wounded on the right, unwounded on the left. The Germans came along our line and pulled out a young Dutchman who was with us. He was a member of the Resistance and had fought right through with the British, getting both arms badly burned when he tried to pick up a phosphorus bomb which had landed in our positions. He was forced to his knees and shot through the back of the neck. The lifeless body slumped to the ground, the heavily bandaged hands sprawled out in front like two grotesque paddles. The German officer who did this said to us, 'That is how we deal with traitors in the Third Reich.' Stunned, we lay on the cold pavement and waited.

A young German soldier began to search the wounded one at a time starting at the far end. He was after arms, ammunition, knives, maps and anything else of military importance. In my experience the ordinary German soldier never took anything off you of intrinsic value such as watches or rings, unlike the British, who would steal anything, even food, off one another. The SS too had different standards, for they not only stole anything of value but tore up photographs and letters, specialising in removing gold fillings from your teeth and even worse. The young German pulled a wallet from one paratrooper's smock but the

Englishman held on to it shouting, 'No, no, give it here, it's mine.'

These were his last words, for his searcher pulled out a pistol and shot him dead. He then looked through the wallet and, finding nothing of military importance, carefully replaced it on the dead body. There was a stupefied gasp from the British. War was one thing but casual murder was another, and we had just witnessed two murders in as many minutes. When the young soldier reached me I had emptied all my pockets and had the contents on my lap ready for his inspection with both arms out by my sides. He held the pistol in his left hand as he rummaged through my belongings with his right. He was curious about the photographs in my wallet and other things but put them all back, frisked me for weapons and remarked in a matter-of-fact voice, 'You do not appear to have anything of military value, but if you have I advise you to get rid of it as you will be searched again and if such items are then found you will be shot.' This was all said in a quiet even tone as if it was the usual routine stuff, which, if anything, added to its menace.

A warning now ran through the German ranks: 'Achtung! Brigade Führer.' A half-track vehicle rumbled into view. Standing next to the driver, his hand on the windshield, was the Hollywood version of a typical Nazi officer, from the tip of his cheesecutter cap, complete with Rommel eyeshield, to his highly polished jackboots. He shouted a lot, expressed his satisfaction at seeing so many wounded British and congratulated everyone in sight. We almost expected him to start dishing out Iron Crosses on the spot but evidently the setting was not quite right, for he ascended his command vehicle and, amid numerous 'Heils', rumbled majestically away.

Once again we were forced to our feet. We hobbled along until we came to a Dutch church, which had been commandeered as a collecting point for wounded prisoners. The church was a modern one with tip-up seats, the backs of which had pockets to contain prayer books. I realised that in my bloodied trouser pocket there were some airborne maps of the Arnhem area. I removed them and stuffed them into one of those pockets, trusting that some patriotic Dutchman would find and dispose of them.

We were hungry and, what was worse, parched with thirst, but neither food nor water was forthcoming that night. We tried to sleep but this was difficult as Jerry kept all the lights on throughout the night. More and more wounded were carried in. My leg ached and smarted but I was past caring, feeling relieved to be in one piece and out of the fighting. Amid all the distractions, and a constant coming and going of German soldiers and Luftwaffe personnel, my head fell forward on my chest. Eventually I dropped off into the dreamless sleep of complete physical exhaustion.

Chapter 7

A PRISONER OF THE GERMANS

THE NEXT morning we woke to find many more paratroopers being brought in, including some of our Machine Gun Platoon along with their fiery little officer. He was in a hell of a temper and proving quite a handful for his captors. It was not long before the Germans organised transport to move us out of Arnhem. All fit men were marched off under heavy guard, presumably to the nearest railway station for removal to prison camp, or Stalag as the Germans called it. Eventually I found myself perched precariously on a one-ton truck with six other airborne wounded. One of these was an airborne artillery bombadier suffering from a spinal wound. He had been placed on a stretcher across the back of the truck, which was open.

The driver and guard were young SS men, who were both arrogant and callous. The guard sat facing us on the folded-down windshield and waved a Luger pistol all the time. These two bully boys were very different from the front-line Wehrmacht soldier; they drove like hell through the streets, being particularly enraged by the encouraging waves, smiles and V-signs we received from Dutch civilians, which only made them go faster. By this time the bombardier was in agony and one of the wounded sitting up behind me nudged me in the back and said, 'Tell that bastard to go easy.' I tried remonstrating with the guard but this merely resulted in threats, while the driver reacted by pushing his foot well down on the floorboard.

When we reached the outskirts of the town the speed eased off slightly although we were still doing about forty as we headed for the open country. The backseat driver nudged me again and whispered in my ear, 'How about jumping the bastards?' This would have been suicidal in view of our condition, especially that of the bombardier, and the speed of the vehicle.

We skidded to a standstill outside a large hospital and the bombardier was off-loaded. Then we continued to race around the Dutch countryside, dropping off first one and then another until there were only three of us left. We began to feel nervous, as the two SS men were obviously getting bored with their assignment and we did not want to end up in a ditch with a bullet in the head, shot 'while attempting to escape'.

We drove up to another hospital. Outside were a large number of wounded German soldiers as well as some fit ones. Much to our surprise the SS men left the vehicle and went into the hospital, leaving us unguarded, except for the fact that we were in the middle of some two hundred Germans.

We saw an olive-drab bus filling up with German wounded. As it appeared obvious that this hospital was also overcrowded and wishing to get away from our two SS men, we hobbled over to the bus and clambered in with the regular German Army wounded. We received some odd looks from them but they did not object to our presence; they seemed more curious about us than anything else. The driver, a civilian, stoked up the boiler at the back of the bus, climbed in, and away we went, no doubt leaving two very puzzled SS men behind us.

Opposite me sat a German in a bright green uniform holding one of his hands and moaning in pain as he rocked to and fro. He received scant sympathy from the chunky apple-cheeked blonde soldier sitting next to me, who nodded in his direction and remarked to me in English, 'He's just a bloody policeman who got in the way.' The speaker was about my own age, wounded in the arm and anxious to talk. There was no animosity – he might have been a member of my own platoon. He told me that the Germans admired the British but despised the Americans, to which I replied that we admired the Germans but despised the Italians. 'So do we,' he chuckled.

He expressed amazement that we had allied ourselves with Uncle Joe, and this point was put to me repeatedly during my captivity. The Germans regarded the Russians as bears that walked like men and saw themselves as the shield of western civilisation against the Bolshevik hordes. I did not like to tell him that I was relying on these same hordes to rescue me, having lost a bit of faith in the ability of my own side to do so. He asked my opinion of German weapons, and was delighted at my praise of the MG34, the Schmeisser and the German mortars. I mentioned the terrific bombardment we had undergone. He laughed and said, 'You should have been where I was.'

Abruptly he asked, 'Who is going to win the war?' – an awkward question – but another German further down the bus turned and shouted, 'The Americans of course!' amid general laughter. The young German offered me a smoke, which I declined, being a non-smoker, and he then took out a battered wallet from which, with difficulty, he extracted some photographs. These were of girls, and some of the photographs included him in quite amorous clinches.

He told me that German photographers usually took such poses of soldiers with their sweethearts. As he passed the snapshots to me he tabulated his collection with the name of the town where the young lady under review resided: 'Frankfurt . . . Mainz . . . Hanover . . .' he murmured, 'Cologne . . .' I told him the Americans were reported there, so he had 'had that one', whereupon he shrugged his shoulders and passed me others: 'Celle . . . Lubeck . . . ' and so on.

Evidently for a well set-up German soldier garrison duty in the Third Reich had its compensations. It was really quite pleasant bowling along the straight Dutch roads in the autumn sunshine in good company, admiring a succession of photographs of amply endowed blondes. I could not help wondering, however, about air attack from our planes. This was noticeably lacking during the battle but was now to be an ever-constant threat to our survival. With the Allies' absolute command of the skies nothing that moved by road, rail or river was safe from their attentions.

We arrived at Apeldoorn and turned into an imposing driveway leading to the Soestdijk Palace, the summer residence of the Dutch royal family, a magnificent building. This was now a front-line military hospital run by SS medical staff and guarded by the picked troops of the Herman Goering Regiment of the Luftwaffe.

We slumped down on the grass and waited. An elderly SS medical orderly appeared. He smiled at us and repeated over and over again the words, 'For you the war is over.' It was all the English he knew and the only answer we received to the questions we put to him.

Eventually an officer emerged and, after saying farewell to our Wehrmacht travelling companions, we were taken to a room, where we were surprised to find about fifty airborne wounded from other elements of the Division, though there were none from my battalion. The room was dominated by a large photograph of Fat Hermann. An orderly came in with a bucket of coffee, which tasted delicious; I was surprised to discover that it was made from acorns. After this we were made to strip and take a shower. We were given no assistance at all by the German medical staff, who just stood about and laughed at our attempts to balance on one leg and wash while trying to keep our bandages dry.

Our bloodstained uniforms were carefully labelled and we were issued with pyjamas. Then we were ushered upstairs to a large thickly-carpeted room, the walls of which were hung with oil paintings. Mattresses were placed on the floor and we were given sheets, a luxury practically unknown in the British Army at that time, as well as thick fleecy blankets, which were also far superior to anything back home. A Dutch civilian in morning coat and striped trousers surveyed our arrival with distaste and kept clucking like an old hen. The paratroopers shouted to him, 'Hey, Joe! How about some mungey, conner. Savvy? What's the matter with the stupid old sod, doesn't he understand English?' The elderly palace official looked at us in horror until an ob-scene but all-too-commonplace airborne expression sent him scurrying away and we never saw him again.

The SS medics brought us a first-class meal of different kinds of cold meat, lettuce which had been really cleaned, tomatoes, new potatoes, black bread and real butter. Some of the men found the black bread unpalatable and threw it away, though a few weeks later they would be giving their wedding rings for a three-kilo loaf of that same despised food. We also received hot coffee and there was plenty of sugar, a bar of chocolate each, some boiled sweets and six cigarettes. All in all it seemed too good to be true. The Dutch civilian cooks in the palace kitchen sent us some English books and papers and even a game of Monopoly. I opened a copy of the *Illustrated London News* and was delighted to find an aerial photograph of Brighton. I could pick out the Pavilion, the lanes, and even my own house. I was very grateful to that unknown Dutchman who gave me that link with home when I needed it so desperately.

The first night in the palace we dozed off to the rumbling lullaby of the guns of the Second Army, which was still trying to break through to our comrades trapped in the 'Cauldron' at Oosterbeek. 'It's not for long,' we thought.

With the exception of a Scot suffering from a particularly painful shoulder wound most of us slept pretty well as we had full bellies for the first time since we had landed in Holland. The next morning we awoke to a routine familiar the world over in hospitals. At about nine we were taken downstairs under our own steam to a large room near the front entrance where we sat on hard chairs. In the centre of the room was an operating table and over the door a large oil painting of Hitler. In one corner a sour-faced SS clerk took down details of our wounds; we were forced to go over to him for this chore.

The door opened and an immaculate German officer appeared, together with a retinue which included a rather pretty blonde nurse. The paratroopers began to sit up and take an interest in life again. The officer and his entire party turned to face the portrait of the Führer and, holding their right arms out stiffly in the Nazi salute, shouted 'Heil Hitler!'

We all burst out laughing and someone blew a raspberry, which infuriated them, not because they were fanatical Nazis but because they had been told to do this by the SS to impress us. The doctor, for that is what the officer turned out to be, removed his peaked cap, gloves and tunic, and donned a white smock, which made a sinister combination with his jackboots. He picked up a pair of forceps and beckoned to the first patient, who hobbled across the room and climbed stiffly on to the operating table.

At this time the Germans were desperately short of anaesthetics, indeed of all medical supplies, so the very minimum was used. The airborne soldier twisted and moaned under half-deadened pain as the sweating MO dug for the bullet or fragment of shrapnel. One after another we were dealt with, being forced to watch the agony of our comrades. Eventually it was my turn to climb on to the table, but despite the size and appearance of my wounds the doctor seemed unimpressed. 'It will heal from the inside. Ja, you will find the flesh will soon grow again. You like football, eh?'

He motioned me to get down from the table and an orderly bound up my leg with paper bandages. By the time we were upstairs again these bandages were sodden and I had to keep turning them round the wound. All in all, though, life at Soestdijk was not too bad and we were quite well treated. Our chief SS orderly was a tall, grey-haired and rather distinguished-looking man called Bernhardt. He spoke excellent English, having at one time been a commercial traveller in the Southampton area. He had served in the First World War and must have been in his mid-forties. He had a rather cynical outlook on life but was excellent at his job and always treated us fairly.

One night eleven paratroopers escaped. The escape was carried out in close collaboration with the civilian staff in the kitchens, some of whom were in the Resistance. We let a fire hose down from a side window, and reeled it up again after the men had vanished into the surrounding trees. They had to dodge the guards of the Hermann Goering Regiment, who were patrolling the ground in camouflage capes and carrying submachine guns: no mean feat for wounded men. We heard that the paras reached the Allied lines within a week.

When the Germans discovered that they had gone there was a great uproar and we were told that we would all be punished individually. Nothing came of this except that we had our cigarette ration docked for a couple of days. I believe the SS medical staff were secretly amused over this slip-up by the Luftwaffe. The guards were doubled as a result and we were forbidden to look out of the window. I tested this one day and stepped back hurriedly as a Lufwaffe soldier unslung his carbine and brought it up to aim.

We were told that we were to be moved to an all-British hospital just a few kilometres up the road. The morning of the move I reported as usual to the surgery, where Bernhardt dismissed the orderly and began to dress my leg himself. 'How old are you?' he asked. 'Nineteen.' Bernhardt shook his head and muttered my age in his own language. I noticed the thorough job he was making of my dressing. He was taking great care, using best quality bandages, not paper, and he even fitted me out with an alloy leg splint which he bound again with stronger bandages. 'Seems a lot of fuss for a few kilometres,' I said. He gave me an 'old-fashioned look' and remarked, 'You cannot be too careful in Holland – there is grave danger of tetanus, however small the journey.'

For lunch we received the best meal we would see until freed; for some of those with me the last good meal they would ever have. I exchanged my pyjamas with an officer who had a nightshirt – he wanted to be in the next planned escape. (He was in it, but none of them made it back to our lines). As I was about to quit the room the Scot with the painful wound sank into his bed, the white sheets and blankets rapidly becoming stained with blood. Several nurses rushed to his assistance and the guards bundled us out.

Downstairs we waited in a corridor while our torn and bloodstained battledresses were re-issued to us for the journey. My boots had been stolen, so I had to hobble over the cobbles to the waiting bus as best I could. The guards who now took charge of us were much older than any we had seen previously. They were sick and embittered by the bombing and the loss of their sons in the war. Sitting in the bus and listening to the excited chatter around me I was surprised how many of our lads still believed that they were being transferred to an all-British hospital. Looking back as we moved off we could see two figures on the steps of the palace waving to us, one being Bernhardt and the other a glider pilot who had succeeded in fooling an SS psychiatrist that he was mentally deranged and not fit to be moved. He aimed to escape and thought that he would have more chance while still in Holland among a friendly civil population than in a heavily guarded Stalag in Germany.

The bus rattled into the town and turned into the railway goods yard. There was a huge groan as we sighted the 'All-British Hospital', a long line of squalid cattle trucks into which wounded airborne soldiers were now being forced. There were forty men to a truck and no rations of any kind except a jug of water. At the very last moment before we commenced our rail journey a man was thrust into the truck, obviously very ill and wearing only his pyjamas. He had pneumonia, so we swept every bit of straw to one to end to make up a bed for him and we all took off our smocks to give him some sort of covering. Amazingly he was to survive a journey which turned out to be a nightmare.

The train suddenly gave a convulsive leap forward, which earned it the title of the 'Kangaroo Express'. We huddled together for warmth but the cold night air penetrated every crack in the floor and sides of the truck. Every jolt was agony, especially for the more seriously wounded. Early in the journey three glider pilots in the next truck made an attempt to escape. They had cut a hole in the roof, using the small ingenious escape saws which we had hidden in our clothing, a feat in itself when one realises the thickness of the wood. Suddenly all hell broke loose as the train jerked to a halt. Two of the pilots managed to jump clear as soon as they were spotted, but the third was hit by machine-gun fire. We heard him cry out, then roll across the roof and fall down on the track. It was terrible to hear his moans and to listen helplessly to the commotion made by the guards as they ran up to him. There was the unmistakable click of a rifle being cocked, then a shot rang out and the moans ceased.

The Germans threw open the doors and shone their torches in our faces. Outside we could see the stabbing beams of searchlights sweeping the surrounding area and we heard the excited baying of tracker dogs. An officer appeared in the open doorway. 'Three of your comrades have attempted to escape. I do not intend to hold this train up all night and if the other two are not recaptured within three minutes one in every three of you will be shot.' There was an incredulous gasp but we had to laugh when a Cockney shouted in a highly indignant voice, 'Ere, you can't do that. It's against the Geneva Convention.' Even the German officer turned away to hide his laughter. One of the escapers was hiding under a nearby truck, and on hearing this threat gave himself up; a guard dog caught the other before he had gone very far. Both men were no doubt roughed up before being shoved back in their truck. We had to wait while the guards nailed fresh planks and barbed wire over the top before going on.

No sooner had we started again than a very young officer of ours and a sergeant, both I believe from the 1st Battalion, also tried to saw a hole through the side of the truck, but there was such an uproar from the rest of us that they were forced to give up the attempt. Neither of these men was wounded and we did not see why we should get shot because of them. They were told to wait until their escape attempt did not put other people's lives in jeopardy.

One night we were strafed by a lone aircraft which, it was thought, was a Mosquito of the RAF. One reason for this assumption was the persistence of the attack, another that it was a two-engined job. Luckily it was armed only with machine guns. Nevertheless it was a most alarming experience, too much indeed for one of the few able-bodied men in the truck, a Canadian, who completely lost control of himself and jumped all over the wounded, crying and hammering on the door to be let out. He caused a great deal of unnecessary suffering before an airborne corporal managed to calm him down.

After two days we were let out in a siding to relieve ourselves. As I squatted down awkwardly an old German guard stood over me with rifle and bayonet; the bayonet was about two inches from my neck and his finger was on the trigger. He was trembling with fear and at every move I made he jerked like a marionette, so I appealed to a tougher-looking individual who understood English to explain to him that I wanted to perform a natural function, not reach for any hidden weapon.

The scenes down the train were truly terrible. Many of the wounded had already died as a direct result of the journey, but the Germans refused to remove them as the commandant of the Stalag would have to sign for so many bodies. Whether or not they were dead or alive did not matter to the Teutonic mind. There was only one airborne MO to cope, aided by three medical orderlies. As we were stopping for no longer than half an hour they had to try and get along the whole length of the train in that time. Consequently there were some ugly incidents when men tried to persuade them to spend more time with their particular comrades, but the medics did their level best to carry out an impossible task.

We were shoved back in and resumed the journey. After four days of hell we reached Hanover, which was only about a hundred miles from Apeldoorn. We peered through the cracks in the truck to catch a glimpse of our first large German city but all we could see were ruins. An air raid siren wailed and we were shunted into a siding. We heard the engine uncouple and chug off down the track. To our horror we discovered that we had been left beside a train of petrol trankers. In the distance we could plainly hear the roar of the approaching Allied bombers; our thoughts over the next ten minutes can be imagined. However, it was not Hanover's turn that day so we were not bombed or burned to death.

We reached Fallingbostel about four that afternoon. The doors were flung open and we saw sunlight and smelt fresh autumn air. The guard rousted us out of the trucks and all the fit and walking wounded were pushed and jostled on to the road. The dead were off-loaded and left in a heap on the platform. The guards begun to count the exhausted men, some of whom were nearly in a state of collapse. Stalag XIB was about a mile away, up a hill. Despite having my leg in a splint I was classed as fit to march, but when passing the open door of a truck I saw some airborne soldiers on stretchers. On learning that they were amputation cases I quickly occupied an empty stretcher and covered myself up. An order was given and the 'fit' were marched off towards the camp. A young German soldier saw us and sidled over; he was obviously on leave. He never said anything but as he went past he flung in a handful of cigarettes, which I collected and distributed.

A guard appeared and demanded to know why we had not paraded with the other men. One of the paratroopers pulled aside his blanket to reveal the stump of his missing leg. The guard flushed and hurried away to find transport, while we lay there and dozed in the warm sun. Eventually a rickety old ambulance arrived with red crosses painted on its sides. We were loaded on but the stretchers were not secured in any way. We had to hold on to one another and to the sides of the truck to prevent ourselves sliding out. On the way to the Stalag we passed the walking wounded who, despite their terrible condition, gave us a cheer. I felt a bit ashamed as many of the men in that marching column were in a worse state than I was, but already I was acquiring the attitude necessary for survival.

When we reached the crest of the hill we could see the camp on the left-hand side of the road. It was enormous. Opposite it were the barracks of a panzer grenadier training regiment and the Stalag guards' married quarters. We drove through huge wooden outer gates past watchtowers manned by alert machine gunners. Stalag XIB was a complex of lagers containing thousands of men of different nationalities: Russians, Poles, Yugoslavs, Italians, French, Americans and British. Before the war it had been a concentration camp and there was a rumour that thirty thousand Russian dead had been buried there in mass graves following a typhus epidemic in 1943.

We stretcher cases were loaded on to ingenious two-wheel trolleys which could be pushed along by one man. Then we were left lying outside a large hut, the camp theatre, in a fine drizzle which had just commenced. The theatre was being used as an interrogation centre. Eventually we were forced to get up, stagger inside and stand in front of a table at which sat three Germans, who proceeded to ask for information. Other Germans went through our pockets. A South Staffs airborne officer who strongly objected to this treatment was slapped repeatedly across the face by a German sergeant-major. After about an hour of this we were taken to the lazarette or camp hospital, which consisted of about eight squalid huts grouped on either side of a red brick road. We were dumped in the corridors of the huts and just left there. We had to make our way into a hut, sort out a bed and also try to help those worse off than ourselves. We put the badly wounded in the lower bunks and also those who had rubber pipes in them dripping pus. The smell was indescribable.

Someone in our hut was scrubbing the floor: it was an English padre. He organised a meal of hot soup and scrounged biscuits off the Yugoslavs as we did not come on to the official ration strength until the following day. He told us that his name was Gedge and that he had been taken at Dunkirk. The Germans allowed him to visit several camps, some better and some worse than Stalag XIB. One can judge the size of his parish by the fact that we only saw him about twice again during the next six months. I never heard Padre Gedge mention religion but then he didn't have to for he was a sterling example of the sort of man we should like to have been. He tried his best to clean us, feed us and inform us, these being our paramount needs.

Those first nights in the lazarette were unforgettable. Everyone seemed to be going through his own special nightmare over and over again. Men tossed and turned in their battle-haunted dreams, men who had fought and held on against great odds until food, water and then ammo had finally run out, men who had seen their officers and NCOs picked off one by one and their mates killed beside them. Listening to the ravings of the wounded, one might well have thought that the battle was still going on. It was like watching a movie over and over again. I began to wonder if some men would ever get over it.

However, we all, or nearly all, quickly adapted ourselves to life in the lazarette. And I met one paratrooper named Shackleton from the 10th Battalion who was to become a lifelong friend. 'Shack', as we called him, was as tough and sometimes stubborn as only a Yorkshireman can be, but this was tempered by a philosophical outlook on life and a great sense of humour. He always had a broken old pipe clenched between his teeth even when there was nothing in it, and he loved to lie back and observe his fellow men. There was plenty of time for this in the Stalag, and all airborne types were 'characters'.

The second day we were in camp a glider pilot was shot dead from one of the watchtowers because he continued to sit in the sun when there was an air raid siren sounding. If we were too

MISSING AT ARNHEM
Brighton Man A P.O.W.

Mr. and Mrs. J. L. Sims, of 111 Hollingbury-road, Brighton, have received news from the War Office, t h a t their son. Para-trooper James William Sims, who was re-ported missing at Arnhem, is a prisoner of war in XI.B Stalag Camp, Germany.

Ptpr. J. W. Sims

"Jimmy" was b o r n in Shef-field, and came to live in Brigh-ton in 1935. He w a s educated at the Ditch-ling-road and Intermediate schools, and after leaving school joined the 15th Sussex Home Guard. previous to joining the Royal Artillery from which he volunteered for the Paratroops.

Before joining the Army he was an assistant with Messrs. Dutton & Thorowgood. East-street, Brighton.

Cutting from the *Sussex Daily News*, 21 November 1944

slow at pulling up the blackout boards at night the Germans fired through the walls of the hut.

Our food each day was as follows:

Breakfast   A cup of acorn coffee.

Dinner   Half a pint of watery soup and three small potatoes.

Tea   A cup of rose-leaf tea, one slice of sour black bread, a minute portion of telemargarine, and a spoonful of ersatz jam complete with wooden pips.

We did not receive Red Cross parcels for the first month and when they did arrive it was only one parcel among four prisoners. The Canadian parcels were the best for quality and ease of division. The American ones had the most in them, including a hundred Lucky Strike or Camel cigarettes and even vitamin pills. Cigarettes, chocolate, soap and certain tinned foods could be traded with the guards or trusty prisoners such as the French, Yugoslavs and Italians; for example, twenty cigarettes might be bartered for one small loaf. In this way we managed to stay alive.

The British parcels were disappointing. Nearly everything in them needed cooking, which was not easy in a Stalag, and no one seemed to have realised that a parcel might have to be divided. Imagine the difficulties of sharing out and holding on to one-fourth of a tin of treacle or sardines; nor can one make porridge with cold water. Moreover the Germans pierced the tins before issue to prevent our stockpiling food for an escape. They would turn the British parcels upside down, with the result that treacle from the bayoneted tins would run like glue over the contents. This would then freeze in a solid mass, along with the sawdust and shavings which were used in the packing. However, we were so hungry that we would eat the frozen concoction as though it was a block of toffee. Fires were not allowed and, fuel being virtually non-existent, we were forced to pare down our beds. The parings were used only for cooking, not for providing warmth. Despite the approach of colder weather and lack of food, morale was very high in the lazarette, but we heard grim tales of the lager to which those judged 'fit' were transferred.

One could see this lager from the hospital. When we arrived

at the Stalag it was occupied by Polish patriots from General Bor's underground army, which had been crushed in the revolt against the Germans at Warsaw about the same time as we had been fighting at Arnhem. I used to stand and watch some really handsome Polish girls playing netball. One day as the first snows of winter fell the SS came for them. They were all well-dressed women. Some even had babies in their arms and a lot had fur coats. All of them, from the oldest to the babes in arms, wore the red and white armband of Poland. What happened to them all? The British took over the lager and we heard that conditions there were dreadful. One day I saw some men from a Scots regiment demonstrating against the death of one of their sergeants through the neglect of the enemy. They charged the barbed wire fencing holding his body aloft on a truckle bed as though it was a banner. In the Stalag the Scots reverted to the sort of behaviour which must have made Hadrian decide to build his wall.

After some weeks I was called for interview by the German commandant to see if I was fit for the lager. This was only a formality, like a Ministry of Pensions medical, for it made no difference what state you were in, you automatically went down there. Some of my wounds were still open and remained so throughout my captivity as we did not get enough food. The office was almost hygienically clean. While I was waiting there a British doctor came in with a death certificate which required the commandant's signature. The British had entered the cause of death as 'Malnutrition' but this was deleted by the cynical old devil, who insisted that 'In the Third Reich there is no such thing as malnutrition.' He then substituted his own reason, which was accepted, under protest, by the MO.

One morning I saw some members of my battalion under the command of the RSM pulling a handcart along with a plain pine coffin on it. Behind the cart were two men carrying a huge wreath of laurel and pine with a large golden ribbon adorning it; this had obviously been made from one of our nylon identification scarves, which were used for calling in air support. Later I learned that it was the funeral of my own platoon officer, Lieutenant Woods, who had been wounded in the lung at

Arnhem and had died as the result of the terrible journey to the camp. This was yet another needless death.

When the day came for me to go down to the lager, Shack arranged for me to team up with a mate of his, Herbie Monk, who hailed from the West Country and was a useful comrade in a place like the Stalag. I spent the first night on a hut floor in the lager and felt things dropping on to my face. The next morning I found that they were lice, and, like every other man in the lager, I was soon fighting an endless battle with these pests. A daily delousing even in the most freezing weather meant that you might keep the number on you down to as few as six. The weaker you were the more you seemed to get.

Herbie and I met up with two other paras, Ted, a trooper from Worthing, and John, a gunner from Woolwich. There were occasional clashes of temperament but Herbie held us together, and we never quarrelled over essentials such as the division of food or what we would trade that month. The conditions in Stalag XIB were appalling even for the most hardened troops and worse than some, particularly the Americans, could face. There were four huts lying on a slight gradient, the Americans having the bottom one and the British and Canadian the top three. When it rained the camp was a sea of mud, and the guards often kept us standing for an hour in the freezing rain just to be bloody when we had a roll call, which was first thing in the morning and at teatime. Men would collapse on parade and often died as a result of being forced to attend it. Medical attention of any sort was virtually unobtainable and anyone taken really ill just died. Indeed, the funerals each day became a sort of relief in the monotony of Stalag life.

The British and Canadians stood the Stalag the best and the Americans the worst, their NCOs seeming quite incapable of exercising any form of discipline in conditions in which discipline was essential to survival. The British and Canadians were lucky in that they had RSM Lord. This extraordinary man was without doubt one of the best regimental sergeant majors the Guards or the British Army for that matter have ever produced. He had at one time been a Brighton policeman, had served as a Guardsman and was at this time Regimental Sergeant Major of the 3rd Battalion, The Parachute Regiment. He created order out of chaos, gave us back our self-respect, treated the Germans with contempt and bullied them into improving conditions. He warned us about the hazards of our overcrowded environment and encouraged us to get out of our huts and exercise. We responded, grumbling as usual, but there is no doubt that without this fine soldier there would have been far more British graves in Stalag XIB than there were.

Christmas 1944 came and went, celebrated with rare gusto under such conditions; morale remained high despite the much-publicised German push in the Ardennes. As soon as it was halted we knew Jerry was nearly beaten – but could *we* still hold out? By this time some of us were in a bad condition.

Shack came down to the lager early in 1945 and we had some get-togethers. The pace of the war outside was speeding up again. In March about a hundred of us were herded to one side after roll call, marched down to Fallingbostel station and entrained. We had no idea why this was done or where we were going. The terrible uncertainty of a prisoner-of-war's life was something he had to adapt to or go mad; for some men the latter was their release from the horror they saw around them. We were taken down the line to a small station which had been hit by rocket-firing Typhoons of the RAF. They had also caught a mixed train of fuel tankers and passenger carriages with shocking results. In a nearby field some SS men were towing the wrecked locomotive away, using a Tiger tank, which gives some idea of the strength of these monster panzers of the German Army. In a ditch lay what remained of the charred bodies of human beings piled one on top of another.

We were forced to clear the damaged track in order that the skilled German railway workers could repair the line. It was raw wet weather and all we had to eat was half a pint of swede soup at noon, which we were forced to consume on the march, no time off being allowed for meals. Our guards were old and miserable; some of them had lost sons on the Russian front and families in the dreadful bombing. One day a chance remark by a Belgian POW sent one old guard berserk. He had lost all his family in an air raid and had to be restrained by the German

NCOs. I was beaten up myself whilst on this job by one of the many Poles serving in the Wehrmacht. At the time I was trying to shelter under the wheel of an overturned wagon to eat my 'skilly' – the paratroopers' name for the watery soup which formed our staple diet.

No sooner was this job completed than the Germans formed a much larger Kommando of about three hundred men. John and I were among those chosen although we were both still suffering from the effects of our wounds as well as from malnutrition. However, we were not sorry to see the back of Stalag XIB. The Kommando offered fresh sights and sounds, and maybe a chance to escape. On the way down to Fallingbostel station we passed some tough little men from a British rifle regiment who were being brought in, and they told us that the Allies had crossed the Rhine. This was great news and we all cheered, which made the Jerries mad. After an uneventful journey we arrived, in the middle of the night, at a much larger town. As we were marched through it we made as much noise as we could, shouting 'Wakey wakey!' and anything else we could think of to annoy our hosts.

We were put in a very large barn-like building on the outskirts of the town, which had a cobbled road running through it and piles of straw on either side. We had to sleep in this and soon found it to be lousy. The town turned out to be Uelzen, an important railway junction which had only recently been bombed. Our job was to clear the damaged track and we slogged away at this from 7am to 7pm, getting even less food than in the Stalag. Yet it was much better than being in camp because there was so much to see: the activity of an enemy town in wartime as well as the constant arrival and departure of overcrowded trains, many well marked with bullet holes. Everyone seemed to wear a uniform of some kind. The German civilians either adopted a reserved attitude towards us or were downright hostile, several even throwing bricks at us as we marched to work. Among the railway workers there were some who were quite friendly, especially the engine drivers, who could always be relied on to give us a saucepan of hot water if we wanted it in a hurry.

One morning while marching to the railway we heard cat-calls and wolf whistles from the head of the column. The cause of this commotion was a really fabulous blonde, clad only in a negligee, who was seated at her dressing table combing her hair in full view of all. She turned out to be the mistress of the local Gauleiter and evidently complained of our behaviour, as after that we went to work by a different route.

One or two escape attempts were made at this time but they were completely unplanned seizures of opportunity by the people concerned. None of them was successful and the escapers were rigorously dealt with by those who recaptured them. It was quite impossible to hoard food for an escape attempt, and most of us now were in such poor physical condition that it was all we could do to drag ourselves to and from work on the rations we were receiving.

Every day the Flying Fortresses of the United States Army Air Forces droned overhead in blocks of thirty or more on their way to targets deep in the heart of the Third Reich. By now the enemy seemed to be able to offer only slight resistance to this aerial onslaught. Although we were guarded by the Wehrmacht, we were directed by German civilian railway officials who, on the whole, were quite a decent crowd. Their one aim in life seemed to be to keep the railway running. The foreman in charge of us had his son helping him; he had lost an arm at Leningrad when the bomber he was piloting was shot down.

Within two weeks all the main lines through Uelzen were clear, and on one particular day there were no fewer than four military trains in the station. Two of these were going to the eastern front, one carrying tanks and the other Dutch and Belgian SS volunteeers. These SS jeered at us while the train was stationary but as soon as it began to move off we pelted them with bricks.

Heading west was a train of youths obviously straight from training camp and the fourth train was packed with wounded from the Russian front. What a target these four trains presented! There was not a bomber in sight, although later in the day a Mosquito circled overhead before making off to the west.

We had just drawn shovels the next morning when a lone

Fortress flew over and dropped a smoke marker right in the middle of Uelzen station. The smoke hung like a huge beckoning finger for the blocks of American bombers fast approaching; I could see the morning sun glinting on their wings. Without any signal being given everyone – civilians, prisoners, guards and SS – started to run for the woods, which were actually in the direct path of the Allied air armada. The German guards were nearly frantic, as some of us had great difficulty in maintaining the pace, but we just managed to reach safety as the first stick of bombs came hurtling down. The ground heaved and trembled under us with each successive explosion. Next to me an SS officer cringed and a German mother tried to soothe her frightened child. The whole area became covered with a pall of yellow dust which even obscured the sun; bits of shrapnel sighed through the wood, clipping off branches and leaves which fluttered to the ground. One B-17 hit by anti-aircraft fire circled lower and lower, belching out black smoke. At each revolution a member of the crew baled out by parachute. We watched the parachutes drift lazily away from us. The crew all managed to escape before it plunged to earth and exploded some way off.

The raid continued all morning. We had no skilly that day and we later heard that the skilly cart had received a direct hit and that over a hundred Allied POWs who had not been able to get away quickly enough had been killed. At last the All Clear sounded and we struggled to our feet. We picked our way through a fantastic lunar landscape where Uelzen railway terminal had once been. Some of the bomb craters were so enormous that they had rolling stock in them. One locomotive was perched on top of a what was left of one of the station buildings. It was quite impossible to recognise our previous surroundings. The SS were swarming all over the area, rounding up wandering civilians and prisoners.

Already the Germans were back at work attempting to create some sort of order out of complete chaos. A truck backed up to an enormous pile of rubble and men wearing grey boiler suits and steel helmets jumped down. They belonged to the Todt Organisation and they cleared the rubble as though their very lives depended on it. I remember thinking that a race that could work like this when all seemed lost would soon put Germany on her feet again once the war was over. As soon as their task was done they shouldered their spades like rifles and marched off singing to their next assignment.

Owing to the tremendous damage inflicted on the railway and the surrounding area the guards decided to take us back to our billet by a roundabout route, as they feared civilian reprisals against us. We saw some Italians being rounded up by SS officers wielding steel-tipped canes. The Italians were cowering in a crater and the SS ordered them out. One Italian had difficulty getting out and kept sliding back. This infuriated one of the SS men, who leapt into the crater and slashed at the Italian's legs. The steel tip tore through the man's thin trousers and his leg spurted blood. He cleared the edge of the crater in a single bound and ran off in terror, pursued by the angry SS officer. The other two SS men collapsed with laughter at this sight and could not understand why we, as fellow Nordics, were not amused.

As we made our way through the outskirts of the town the effects of the American carpet bombing became all too clear. We saw a horse and cart with both the horse and the driver, an old man, lying dead in the road. We saw the bodies of men, women and children who had been killed by the bombing and, worst of all, a shrapnel-riddled pram with a dead baby inside it. The owner of a large house came out and demanded that our guards make us clear up some of the damage. A crowd began to collect, mostly women, and we noticed that our guards looked very uneasy. Some of the women shouted 'RAF Terror Flieger!' and they called out the names of blitzed German cities – 'Hanover-Köln-Hamburg-Berlin.' We retaliated with 'Warsaw-Rotterdam-Belgrade-Coventry-London.' Things began to look nasty as the women converged on us carrying bricks, cooking pots, sticks and carving knives. They were much more terrifying than the SS. Help arrived in the unlikely form of an arrogant Luftwaffe officer. He took charge of the proceedings, mollified the women and screamed at our guards to get us shovelling. 'You will all stay in Germany until every house and every city is rebuilt brick by brick,' he told us. We decided to work and the

Germans hung around watching us while our guards, suitably
encouraged, butted us with their rifles. After about an hour the
crowd lost interest and dispersed, and the Luftwaffe officer
ordered our guards to get us back to our quarters as quickly as
possible.

Following this attack the Germans moved into the vicinity a
flak train commanded by a stocky, good-natured but completely
cynical warrant officer. Red-faced, with a cigar in his mouth,
and his chest covered with decorations, he was a realist. When
asked how long the war would last he replied, 'How fast can
your tanks go?' One day we asked him about his chest-full of
medals, and he told us that he had served in Poland, Norway,
France, Greece and Russia; and in Russia from Leningrad to
Odessa.

'How on earth have you managed to survive?' I asked.
'Simple,' he said. 'They send me to protect a camp, a town or an
oilfield and I always keep my train well in view until I sense an
air raid. This makes me and my crew very popular but as soon
as the bombers are coming we get the hell out of it down the
line – room to manoeuvre, you understand. Here, have a cigar,
Tommy.' His crew was a mixed one and the sexes openly slept
together. 'It's good for them,' said the warrant officer.

In the devastating air raid that Uelzen had suffered a train-
load of civilians had been bombed and hundreds killed. The
Germans wanted to clear the wreckage but did not trust us to
do the job as they knew we would loot the bodies. Instead they
brought in about two hundred concentration camp prisoners,
all dressed alike in striped pyjama-like suits. Each man carried a
long-handled spade and they moved like mindless automatons.
We watched in fascinated horror. The prisoners were chivied
along by some of their own kind who were trusties. These
trusties were armed with rubber truncheons, which they used
again and again on their charges, but the prisoners did not
appear to feel the blows that rained down on them. Could these
shuffling creatures really be men like ourselves? It didn't seem
possible.

As the procession drew near we noticed that all eyes were
focused on one of our men who was cutting himself a slice of

swede. 'Throw them a bit,' whispered someone and he did. Two hundred pairs of eyes tracked that piece of swede's passage through the air like radar. As it hit the ground the stick-like figures were galvanised into life. They fell in a seething scrum on top of that sliver of swede oblivious to the truncheons of the trusties. At first the moronic SS guards laughed at the trusties' failure to restore order, then they lost patience and went in with boot, whip and rifle butt until they had driven the stick men back into some sort of formation. They still had that fixed half-idiot expression on their faces as the trusties lashed them across the shoulders and head with their truncheons in an attempt to gain favour with their SS overlords.

We witnessed another terrible incident not long afterwards. Ten men, wearing striped suits with the yellow Star of David on them, started working on the section of railway line next to ours. They were guarded by one SS man. As the guard marched up and down his beat the ten men kept pace with him like attendant moons, always digging and working but always making sure that they were close to him. They never took their eyes off him although he appeared to pay hardly any attention to them. It was such a strange sight that we asked our guard what was happening. He told us that in concentration camps there was a rule that if you went on an outside working party and strayed more than ten feet from the SS guard you were liable to be shot on the spot. The guard knew this as well as the prisoners and was quite obviously deriving sadistic satisfaction out of his power of life and death over his charges.

One day the Germans took our Kommando up the railway line to a junction which had been damaged in the bombing. The two sets of rails were attached to a solid metal bed. The whole structure, which looked like part of a gigantic toy railway set, was tilted at an angle of nearly forty-five degrees. The Germans said that they wanted us to shift it. We couldn't believe that they were serious for it must have weighed tons. We told them we needed a crane or 'machinery', as they called it. The Germans laughed. 'Ach, yes, Englanders, you are quite right. In the morning we will have machinery.'

The next morning when we reached the railway we could

hear shouts and the crack of whips. What we saw was not only
appalling but amazing. The Germans had brought up Russian
prisoners, most of whom were stripped to the waist and looked
like scarecrows. They stood shoulder to shoulder round the huge
metal junction and were actually lifting it off the ground and
carrying it away from the track. The SS guards were whipping
them and screaming abuse but the Russians seemed oblivious
to this. However starving they were they were not in such a
desperate plight as the concentration camp inmates and you
could see that their spirit was unbroken. As they heaved away
they chanted in Russian – something like 'Heave bar chodi' or
'Heave bar rupka'. Our guards were amused when they saw the
expression on our faces. 'Yes, Englanders. There is our machinery. How do you like it? It's easy to maintain and if it breaks
down we've got plenty more.'

As the Allies advanced we faced another threat from the
skies. This was the American long-range Thunderbolt fighter,
which swept out of the sun at over 400 mph to strafe anything
moving on the roads and railways. Early each morning a two-
engined aircraft carrying a lot of radar antennae regularly took
off from a nearby airfield; it always heeled over when crossing
the railway to have a look at us. It used to fly so low that we
could almost recognise the pilot. One morning it was jumped by
three Thunderbolts and went down in flames.

On another day the Thunderbolts attacked the flak train in
the station and the German warrant officer with most of his
crew joined us in the ditch. As they came in for a second attack
a strapping blonde, who had stayed on the train, leapt to man
the multiple cannons and opened fire on the leading plane. She
was a magnificent sight and quite without fear, and she must
have caught the American plane in the fuel tanks for it simply
blew up. The other planes sheered off. The Germans jumped
from the ditch cheering their Amazon, while the warrant officer
nearly swallowed his cigar. I often wonder how he made out
his log book for that day.

The land war drew nearer and for the first time in eight
months we heard our own artillery and even the distinctive
chatter of a Bren gun. Uelzen became a crossroads for troops

hurrying both east and west to stave off defeat, as well as for refugees from eastern Germany fleeing from the wrath of the Red Army. The place was becoming overcrowded and Hitler ordered all prisoners to be moved to Berlin to be held as hostages. In the second week of April we were marched out of town to the east, passing hordes of civilians fleeing from the Russians, and troops dug in and vigilantly awaiting the enemy from the other direction. There were also many burning vehicles, among them a bus-load of soldiers who were all dead. We had to march through the SS von Clausewitz Panzer Division, which was lined up on each side of the road waiting to go into action. Neat coloured flags marked out HQ and other formations. These SS troops stared at us sullenly and we later found out that they had cut the throats of eleven of our men who had tried to make a last-minute escape as Germany was collapsing.

We left the main road and eventually arrived exhausted at a small village called Vinstedt. Later that day we saw two staff cars belting along the road towards Berlin, perhaps all that was left of the von Clausewitz Panzer Division after being cut to pieces by the British. The Germans were pulling out of Vinstedt. Our senior NCO, a Scots sergeant, advised us for our own good to stick together because, in the fluid state of the front, the SS were executing German soldiers suspected of desertion on the spot and as POWs our chances would be nil if picked up. The Scots sergeant refused to move when ordered and we all sat down. He then suggested to the German guards that they had better hand over their rifles, promising that they would be correctly treated. Without a word the Germans gave us their weapons but about an hour later we had to hand them back when we sighted a detachment of SS heading towards Vinstedt. They had an 88mm gun and were coming to defend the village, until our guards persuaded them that they had already been out-flanked by the British. The SS withdrew and we took over the rifles again.

We moved into a large field and spread out. Shells were falling and some of our men dug slit-trenches, but most of us were incapable of such efforts. On 19 April 1945 we were the astonished spectators of a duel between a Tiger tank and a

British self-propelled gun which entered our field from opposing corners. We hugged the earth as these two leviathans fired over us. Neither scored a crippling blow but the German gave best and backed out, then turned and made off, hotly pursued by the British SP. Both armoured vehicles completely ignored us. The Tiger was picked off by a rocket-firing Typhoon before reaching the crest of a nearby hill.

An Auster artillery-spotting aircraft flew over and we laid out scraps of towelling to spell POW. We waved like mad but the pilot gave no sign of having seen us and sheered off westwards. Later that day we heard a strange noise in the sky. Our jaws dropped in amazement as we saw an aircraft shaped like a cigar, with low wings on which two pods were suspended. None of us at that time had ever heard of jet propulsion and to come across a plane with no propellers shook us all rigid. The guards were delighted at our unease and told us that this was just one of Hitler's many secret weapons which would sweep the Allies back into the sea. Two Thunderbolts dived on what we later discovered was a Messerschmitt 262, the world's first operational jet fighter. The German pilot must have spotted them and opened up the throttle, for when the Thunderbolts reached where he should have been he was miles away. It was a very convincing demonstration of this new form of air power. I wondered just how many of these miracle planes the Luftwaffe had.

We spent an uneasy night full of alarms. I remember that a terrific din was kicked up over a last issue of bread. Next morning we were all standing on the outskirts of Vinstedt looking westward. After a while a solitary Bren gun carrier emerged from the woods opposite and threaded its way cautiously towards us. There was a pregnant pause, then suddenly three hundred cheering prisoners charged towards the carrier. I have often thought that the driver and his officer passenger must have had nerves of steel not to open fire on us, as from a distance it was impossible to tell if we were friend or foe. We practically lifted the carrier off the ground as we engulfed it in a human wave. At last it was all over.

PARATROOP AIRCRAFT MENTIONED
IN THE TEXT

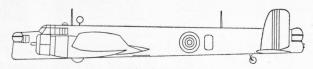

Armstrong Whitworth Whitley Mk III
Span: 84 feet
Length: 69 feet 3 inches
Engines: Two 920 hp Armstrong Siddeley Tiger VIII
Maximum speed: 215 mph

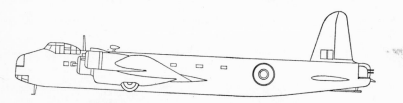

Short Stirling Mk. III
Span: 99 feet 1 inch
Length: 87 feet 3 inches
Engines: Four 1,650 hp Bristol Hercules XVI
Maximum speed: 270 mph

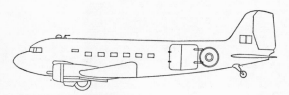

Douglas Dakota C-47 'Skytrain'
Span: 95 feet 6 inches
Length: 63 feet 9 inches
Engines: Two 1,200 hp Pratt & Whitney R-1830-92
Maximum speed: 230 mph

C·V·McCANN.

AIRBORNE INSIGNIA

Parachute Regiment cap badge

Original shoulder title of the 2nd Battalion, The Parachute
Regiment

Wings badge

Divisional flash worn by all airborne troops

Produced by Willet, Walker and Pinfold

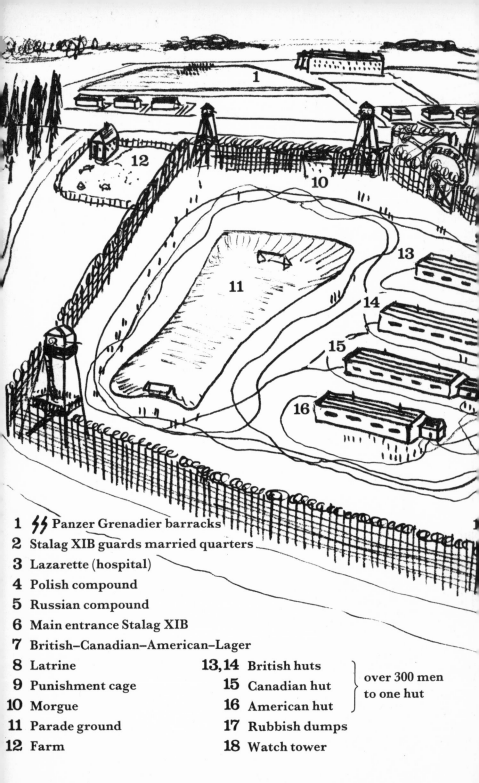

1 ⚡⚡ Panzer Grenadier barracks
2 Stalag XIB guards married quarters
3 Lazarette (hospital)
4 Polish compound
5 Russian compound
6 Main entrance Stalag XIB
7 British–Canadian–American–Lager
8 Latrine
9 Punishment cage
10 Morgue
11 Parade ground
12 Farm

13,14 British huts
15 Canadian hut
16 American hut
17 Rubbish dumps
18 Watch tower

} over 300 men to one hut